Discovering the Individual

Foreword by Lewis Thomas, M.D.

Preface by Kenneth Clark

W · W · NORTON AND COMPANY · INC · NEW YORK

Discovering the Individual

A Fascinating Journey to New Frontiers of Immunology and Genetics

JEAN HAMBURGER, M.D.

Translated by Beatrice Bishop Berle, M.D.

Originally published in France under the title *L'Homme et les hommes*
© 1976 by Librairie Ernest Flammarion

Book design by Antonina Krass
The typeface is Garamond
Manufactured by Haddon Craftsmen

Library of Congress Cataloging in Publication Data
Hamburger, Jean.
Discovering the individual.
Translation of L'homme et les hommes.
1. Human biology—Philosophy. 2. Immunology—
Philosophy. 3. Human genetics—Philosophy.
4. Natural selection—Philosophy. I. Title.
QP34.5.H3513   573.2   77-20215
ISBN 0-393-06433-6
1 2 3 4 5 6 7 8 9 0

Contents

Foreword

It is safe to assert that the general state of human health has never been as good as it is in our society today, nor have the prospects for the future ever seemed brighter. Thanks to the vast improvements over the past half century in public health technology, sanitation, nutrition, and medical therapy (especially the therapy of infectious diseases), the vital statistics for the nation are nothing short of spectacular. More of us survive infancy and enjoy a longer span of life than at any earlier time in human history. We have rid ourselves of what used to be our most frightening plagues. Tuberculosis and tertiary syphilis, the major destroyers a mere forty years ago, are vanishing from our hospitals. And yet there is a paradox. With all the improvement, there has never been a time of such worrying and preoccupation with illness, or the threat of illness. The very word "health" has come to mean, in the public mind, a chancy, unstable kind of holding operation in which, only for the time being, disease is staved off. The health care system has become a vast, expensive symbol for the belief that the human organism is a fundamentally fragile, fallible contraption, always in danger of falling apart, always in need of being propped up by professionals.

There are signs that this societal neurosis, with its own sort of contagion, is spreading in our minds to affect the way we think about the rest of nature. We are beginning to talk despairingly about ecology, and the tremendous ecosystem which comprises the life of the earth, as if the planet were a great clinic filled with vulnerable, failing patients. We are even worried by the prospect that we might, all by ourselves, kill it.

There is a sort of reverse hubris in both these attitudes, and a fundamental lack of respect. The human organism is indeed an intricately made, delicately balanced, incredibly complex mechanism, filled with autonomous working parts which work together by signaling systems beyond our comprehension. The most spectacular thing about it is that it works so well, almost all of the time. It is, like all of life, resilient, resourceful, and fundamentally tough. The rest of nature, viewed as a whole, has the same internal look of complexity, with an infinite number of collaborating working parts, functioning together in a marvelous synchrony. One of the working parts, an important one in our view but perhaps not as vital as we wish to believe, is us.

Professor Hamburger's book provides some illuminating

glimpses of how the whole system works. His method is essentially reductionist, since this is how science gets its information in the necessary detail, but the illuminations come with the exhilarating sighting of *connections*. What you will be reading here is not enough to see the picture whole —centuries more of biological science will be needed before we can hope, if ever, for anything like a whole picture —but there is enough here to demonstrate the existence of connections throughout the system: an organism is like an ecosystem, the organisms contained in ecosystems function like organelles, and the biosphere itself, viewed from a certain distance, is like a single organism. Or, if you like to think about the possibility of connections with life in other galaxies, an organelle.

It is a system that commands respect, and confidence, and something like elation, mixed with insatiable curiosity about the details. All of these feelings are there to discover in this book, in and between the lines.

LEWIS THOMAS, M.D.
President, Memorial Sloan-Kettering Cancer Center, New York

Preface

That scientists and what, for convenience, may be
called humanists should understand each other is one of the
principal needs of the time. The scientists must take the
initiative. For a hundred years they have been in the ascen-
dant. No one can say that literature has improved in that
time, whereas science has made, and is still making, such
enormous strides as to have conquered whole new areas of
life. No humanist would now try to contribute to the subject, as did Goethe and Coleridge. But fortunately many
scientists, from Buffon and Darwin downwards, have written so clearly that their thoughts and discoveries have been
made accessible to the average intelligent reader. In recent
years popularizing scientists like J. B. S. Haldane, Julian

Huxley, and Jacob Bronowski have had an influence on our over-all picture of the world.

Dr. Jean Hamburger is a doctor and a biologist of very great distinction, and he has felt impelled to share some of his conclusions with those who lack scientific training. His book, *Discovering the Individual*, is well written in an apparently simple style, completely free from jargon, and is full of allusions which show the author to be a man of wide culture. But it takes no short cuts, and the first section, in which, through a study of organ transplantation, he proves that each individual is chemically unique, down to the minutest portion of his body, and that this uniqueness is defended by an infinitely complex system, must be read carefully. He then goes on to show how human diversity is the key to the survival of mankind, and that human superiority must be related to the unique structure of the human brain.

Having established the fact that the uniqueness of each individual is not just a whim of nature but plays an essential role in the survival of the species, Dr. Hamburger enlarges his theme from the individual to the problem of man's relations with nature. The belief of Wordsworth and the romantic poets that man's relationship with nature was one of loving participation is now seen to be a myth. In fact Nature is ruthless and terrible. The rules developed through the generous and passionate aspirations of man under the name of ethics reveal more clearly their true significance, which is a revolt against the natural order, a refusal to obey passively the normal law of evolution and survival.

In the last chapter of his book, entitled "Playing with

Fire," Dr. Hamburger illustrates this sentence by examples, of which the saddest and, in the long run, the most alarming is the effect of good medical care and new medicines, which prolong the lives of those who, by the natural law, would have died as children. They grow up, procreate, and so will ultimately lower the whole intellectual and physical level of the community. My only hope would be what Dr. Hamburger calls, after one of his biological experiments, "the thousandth mosquito," who may be a Mozart or a moron, but at least escapes from the general trend. Still, it is clear that to protect the species against the spread of hereditary diseases is contrary to natural law, and is a potential danger to the human race, unless it can be controlled. In a section called "Paying the Piper" he suggests some ways in which this can be prevented, although only by sacrifices.

The last pages of Dr. Hamburger's book are not only an intellectual treat, but are profoundly moving. He knows that in the conflict between natural law and human ethics, it will not be reason, but emotion, that will win the day, and gives as an example the conservation of the blue whale. When reason and international agreement had failed, this was achieved by a surge of mass emotion. In retrospect one realizes that all through the book Dr. Hamburger's rational approach has been supported, or even guided, by his feelings. This fusion of reason and emotion is the mark of the true humanist, and *Discovering the Individual* is a book that will delight all humanists and help to restore their wavering faith.

London   KENNETH CLARK
1977

Introduction

It happened during a vacation in the south of France. There, in the back hills, tourists are still scarce, the air is fragrant with honeysuckle and thyme, and the world seems remote enough to be contemplated with serenity. I was preparing a lecture to be given in New York at the coming International Congress of Transplantation. The organizers had asked me to give a talk on an apparently strange subject: What can research on organ transplantation offer to biology and medicine, *excluding* organ transplantation itself?

At the beginning, the aim of transplantation research had been extremely simple. Young men and women, whose bodies were otherwise perfectly sound, were dying because one of their vital organs—the liver, the heart, the kidneys

—was destroyed by disease. The problem was to find a way to replace this organ. Less than a quarter of a century ago this had seemed only a hopeless dream. But then an unprecedented international effort was launched in an attempt to understand and control the phenomenon of graft rejection. And today men and women have been living with a transplanted liver for six years, a transplanted heart for eight years, or a transplanted kidney for as long as eighteen years.

But this effort, toward an apparently specific goal, had now had the most astonishing destiny. It had led to a series of discoveries in biology and medicine which went far beyond organ transplantation. Mysteries were uncovered in the most varied fields—genetics, ethnology, pathology. New ways of treating or preventing disease were found. New insights into the interdependence between parasites and their hosts were perceived. These were some of the extraordinary discoveries which had sprung from transplantation research and which the Congress had asked me to review.

So I was climbing a footpath in Provence, mulling over my lecture, when I was suddenly startled by the thought that the implications on which I was to comment were not only the concern of the physician and the biologist. They actually led to a new concept of the individual and his relationship to mankind. What was challenged was nothing less than our view of the human venture. These reflections are the subject of the present book.

Are the reflections of a biologist of any use for the conduct of public affairs? Could they help in understanding the ills that afflict human society? Could they even offer remedies?

I believe that scientific investigators should not try to shape policy. Science is no more qualified for such a task than a boatbuilder for shaping the character of a sea captain. Scientists can present facts, they cannot impose a course of action. At most, they can provide information to facilitate decision-making. The biologist and the physician know that in the matter of politics they are in no way superior to other men. They are even afraid of the temptation to slide unwittingly from "what I have observed" to "what must be done."

Yet the devil—the tempter—is there: "You who have spent your life trying to understand the laws which govern human beings, are you not in a better position than common mortals to know what decisions should be made for the good of humanity?"

"Certainly not," the biologist will answer. "Experience has shown that science always gets into trouble when it gets involved in politics. Happy was the time when the only aim of science was to satisfy the curiosity of men. Science was pure then, above controversy. It worked in peace and was respected by all men. The trouble began when science provided society with new tools for action. In the time of Louis XIV, the Marquis de Louvois addressed the Royal Academy of Science in these terms, 'I call investigative research a game which chemists pursue to amuse themselves, I call useful research that which may serve the King and the State.' " So the biologist would continue, "Society today has mixed those two kinds of research so thoroughly that Hiroshima has fouled the study of the atom. Even medicine, which has recently given us the means to cure so many diseases, is called to account. Men will continue to respect science only if science sticks rigidly to its search for knowledge and refuses to compromise itself in influencing the way society makes its decisions."

"You are years behind the times," the tempter will reply. "The matter has already been settled, the fusion of science and society is irrevocable, society provides the funds for science. It is too late to discuss whether science is at fault; the question is whether scientists are conscious of their responsibility to prevent the explosion of knowledge from becoming a catastrophe."

Catastrophe? At the mention of this word, it has become fashionable to try to saddle scientific researchers with guilt. People who play this game are probably also those who find disturbing such achievements of the human mind as austerity, intellectual honesty, the critical examination of data—in sum, the opposite of arrogance—all qualities of the mind fostered by the scientific method. Let us not fall into the trap laid by people playing this game. I believe that the destiny of man is bound up irreversibly and magnificently with the pursuit of knowledge and understanding. I believe that science today is in the process of fulfilling this destiny.

Science today in no way resembles what was once called science. For centuries it was an intellectual exercise where conclusions were reached not through the modest and patient study of facts, but sprang full-blown from the imagination. Neither controls nor doubts were required. The treasure of the human mind that we might call scientific humility was painstakingly brought forth by Western civilization. And now, astonishingly enough, Western civilization behaves like a man who has discovered an extraordinary gem yet quickly becomes so accustomed to it that he forgets its magnificence.

I also believe that men of science are no longer locked inside an ivory tower. They feel not guilty, but responsible. They recognize a new duty—to inform society of the consequences of their discoveries, both useful and pernicious. But their responsibility stops there. It does not require that the scientist impose his own law. I would not have faith in a republic of scientists. Indeed, I believe that scientists would lose the confidence of the people if they abandoned their distance from emotional polemics, their restraint in making affirmations, their refusal to dictate the conduct of human affairs.

This could lead to the conclusion that scientists should only report facts without commentary. Let others reflect, let them go beyond the bare facts to nourish their thoughts if they wish.

But another course is that the scientist does not forget that he too is a human being. And, as such, he too may present personal reflections, pose questions, and even make suggestions, always provided that he does so not as a scientist, but simply as a human being.

In this book I have chosen to pursue the latter course.

Discovering the Individual

CHAPTER **One**

Of Mice and Men

The dream of replacing a diseased kidney or heart by
a new kidney or a new heart has today come true. Tales of
organ transplantation date back to the most ancient times.
The story is told that Pio Tsiao, a Chinese physician living
three centuries before Christ, was endowed with magical
powers. His eyes, he said, were so sharp that they could
perceive the organs within a body, and he declared himself
capable of removing a man's heart and putting another in
its place.

Later, in fifteenth-century Italy, the same ancient dream
haunted painters. In the museums of Italy you can still see
portrayals of the legend of Sts. Cosimo and Damien. The
saints are severing the gangrenous leg of a white man to

replace it with a leg taken from a black man recently deceased.

As late as one hundred years ago people were still writing the most incredible nonsense on the exchange of tissues and organs between animals. Some time ago I was searching for information on the history of organ transplantation when I came across a dusty book entitled *La Greffe animale* (Grafting in Animals). It had been written in 1863 by an eminent member of the Société de Biologie de Paris, Dr. Paul Bert. Imagine my excitement. Here were pages and pages on the subject of transplantation. Imagine also my dismay to find that the book was only a romantic fantasy, except there was nothing romantic about it. Even in those times many physicians still felt that they could write down anything which might emerge full-blown from their imagination, without taking the trouble to verify it. Times have changed. The scrupulous methods of science have finally taken over in medicine and biology.

From Organ Transplantation to the Concept of Individuality

The first significant step in the history of organ transplantation was taken only at the beginning of this century, when a French investigator, Alexis Carrel, described a method by which arteries or veins could be sutured end to end. Dr. Carrel later emigrated to the United States to find better conditions for research. He became a fellow of the Rockefeller Institute and was awarded the Nobel Prize in 1912 for his work on vascular suture and the transplantation of blood vessels and organs.

Dr. Carrel's discovery of an effective way to connect vessels was a milestone. It was obvious that a kidney, a liver, or a heart could not survive in a new body without a blood supply. This blood must go from the body of the recipient to the graft and then return to the recipient. Dr. Carrel's technique made this possible, with a connection between the arteries of the recipient and those of the transplant to bring the blood, and a similar vein-to-vein connection to return it.

So, at this point, the problem was only a question of fine needlepoint. Surgeons expert in this art were not lacking. In 1906, Jaboulay tried to apply this method in France by grafting the kidneys of pigs or goats on the upper arms of women threatened with total kidney failure. But the kidneys did not function. Fair enough, was the comment; a pig or a goat kidney is not a human kidney. A graft cannot succeed if the organ does not come from the same species.

Just at that time a discovery was being made which was to become one of the most important landmarks in the history of modern biology. It was not made overnight. In fact, at first it seemed so astonishing that no one dared to report clearly what he knew for fear of being ridiculed. It took ten years of confusion, hesitation, and tentative interpretations before everyone had to acknowledge the unbelievable but indisputable fact: if the kidney of one dog is transplanted into another dog, or if skin from one mouse is grafted onto another mouse, or if a piece of human skin is grafted to another human, despite the apparent similarity between donor and recipient in each case, the graft is recognized as a foreign body and promptly destroyed.

Conversely, if the tissue or the organ comes from the animal itself and is grafted back in another location (this is called an autograft), it works perfectly—there is no rejection. Similarly, in transplantations between identical twins, whom biologists consider to be but two specimens of the same individual, no rejection occurs.

The significance of these findings is clear. Within the same animal species, be it mouse, rat, dog, or man, apart from identical twins, no two individuals are exactly alike. Grafts between them (called allografts) are always rejected. Each individual is able to recognize another individual of the same species as different from himself, even when they are blood relations. Having identified the allografted tissue as foreign, he destroys and eliminates it, while he recognizes fragments from his own body as his own and does not reject them.

How We Inherit Markers Which Determine Our Individuality

We are endowed at birth, in fact at the moment of conception, with markers of our personality, and these differentiate one individual from every other individual of the same species. These markers form part of a very complicated heritage, since they are handed down through an interminable chain of ancestors. Thus, each living being is unique because he represents the chance encounter between two individuals, each of whom bore a unique set of hereditary characteristics.

Let us imagine an alphabet composed of thousands and

thousands of letters. Let us suppose that out of this alphabet several million letters and words are used to create an individual. One-half of them come from a male, Individual A, and the other from a female, Individual B. If C is the third individual so created, he will in turn mix at random one-half the letters and words which he inherited with half the letters and words inherited by a fourth and different individual, D. Imagine that in man this little game has repeated itself over 35,000 years (if you start from men of the Cro-Magnon period), or even 15 million years (if you begin at the origin of man). Consider then the fine imbroglio, the countless possible combinations, the virtual certainty that with each new mix an entirely original being will be created. The uniqueness of each personality does not reside in the letters and the words themselves, but in their unique combination.

The first paragraph of the Constitution of the United States of America contains approximately 10,000 letters out of our meager twenty-six-character alphabet. How long would it take an illiterate animal (or a computer, for that matter) playing with these same 10,000 letters to arrive at an identical arrangement? Perhaps forever. When the alphabet itself is made up of millions of characters, the number of possible combinations is evidently so great that each of them will be unique.

This is an approximate picture of the making of an individual—whether human or animal. It is as though he were a cutout set against an immense background reaching back hundreds of thousands of years and made up of billions of individuals of the same species. A few examples will bring this picture into better focus.

The Genetics of Individual Markers:
The Major Histocompatibility Complex

Everyone today knows that heredity is based on the transmission of genetic material by chromosomes. Man is endowed with twenty-three pairs of chromosomes, located in
the nucleus of each of the billions of cells which make up
his body. The chromosomes are identical in every one of
these cells. They can be seen through the microscope: as
one cell begins to divide and form two daughter cells, the
chromosome filaments appear, looking like Chinese ideo-
grams. For the past few years, many studies have concen-
trated on one small area of chromosome No. 6 in man and
of chromosome No. 17 in the mouse. This is the area where
the principal control station for the regulation of graft rejection was found to be located. It goes by the name of the
"major histocompatibility complex." (Histocompatibility
means tissue similarity allowing acceptance of grafts.)

Investigation into the relationship between graft rejection and heredity began with the work of Little and Tyzer
on transplantation of breast cancer in the Japanese waltzing
mouse. They noticed that this cancer could be successfully
grafted onto a mouse of the same strain, but that it was
rejected by all other mice. If one of these other mice was
bred with a waltzing mouse, their progeny did not reject the
cancer. But if these first-generation hybrid mice were then
bred with other mice, the following generation did reject
the graft. This method of interbreeding mice soon gener-
ated a mass of information on the transmission of hereditary

characteristics. It led to an important discovery: if mouse siblings are interbred, if the same incestuous breeding is repeated with their offspring, and repeated again through several dozen generations, it eventually gives rise to an artificial strain of mice (improperly named "pure") in which the animals accept grafts from each other without rejection.

This acceptance of grafts was interpreted as evidence that each member of this "pure" strain has eventually inherited identical personality markers, or, if you prefer, identical histocompatibility markers as defined above. One by one these compatibility markers were identified in the mouse through the technique of interbreeding. In a celebrated work published in 1948, an Englishman, Gorer, and two Americans, Lyman and Snell, demonstrated that the most important histocompatibility markers depend on a very precise area in the chromosome. They labeled this area "locus H2." Since that time, more ink has been spilled in discussing this minute area than in describing the planet Mars. We shall see why.

H2 Markers in the Mouse

The importance of the H2 area in the mouse was quickly recognized because of the part it plays in the rejection of grafts. The rejection of grafts is more or less strong, depending upon the degree of dissimilarity between the H2 areas of the donor and the recipient of a graft. This is easy to understand: on the surface of every cell of the graft donor lie markers whose structure has been coded by the

H2 area in the seventeenth chromosome. The graft is recognized by the recipient as more or less different from its own H2 personal markers, and the greater the difference the stronger the response leading to rejection.

Let me add that a method for determining which H2 markers an individual mouse possesses was soon discovered. Shortly thereafter, the same method was extended to all animals, including man. This method is called *typing.* The principle is simple. If, for instance, one injects white blood cells from a mouse into another mouse with a different H2, the injected mouse reacts against the alien markers by manufacturing antibodies, that is, substances resulting from an immunization process. The structure of these antibodies is well known today—they are called immunoglobulins. We will have occasion to discuss them later. These antibodies are so well adapted to the alien markers which induce their formation—so *specific,* to use the technical term—that they may be employed to detect the presence or the absence of these same markers in a third mouse. For those interested in the procedure, here in brief is how it is done. Blood cells from the animal to be typed are submitted to a series of antibodies corresponding to different known markers. A chemical system known as Complement, extracted from blood, is added. Complement is a cell killer which is active only when the antibody meets the corresponding marker on the cell. If the cells survive, one can conclude that they do not possess the tested marker; if they die, they do possess it.

HLA Markers in Man

The same method is applicable to the study of man. It is now possible to draw a detailed map of the distribution of these markers among the human population. Like mice, the human species has a major histocompatibility area in its genetic material. This area also contains other fascinating genes, which will make their appearance in the coming pages. The human major histocompatibility area, corresponding to the H2 area in the mouse, is called HLA. *H* stands for human, *L* for leukocytes (the white blood cells on which the first known histocompatibility marker was described by Jean Dausset), and *A* designates this specific area, paving the way for the use of subsequent letters of the alphabet to identify other areas as they come to light.

More than seventy different HLA markers have now been identified. Every individual has his personal set of HLA markers labeling each cell of his body. Half of them were inherited from his mother and half from his father. Just with the HLA markers identified so far, more than 980,000 different sets are theoretically possible. Obviously, this is already sufficient for two individuals to stand little chance of being chemically identical. We will see later that this probability is further reduced to zero because the same variability (or, to use the technical term, the same genetic polymorphism) is found in innumerable other molecules also coded through heredity.

Other Genes in the Same Chromosomal Area

A gene is the unit through which an inherited message is transmitted. A chromosome is made up of thousands of different genes. In addition to the genes responsible for the H2 markers in the mouse, at least a thousand other genes are located in the same area. The inventory of these genes has hardly begun, but the early results are already very exciting. They demonstrate the importance of the tiny H2 area in genetic polymorphism, that is, in differences between individuals. For instance, the H2 area contains genes coding the structure of various substances found in the blood. One of these is Complement, the killing substance referred to above (see page 32), and another is a protein called Ss, or "seric substance," discovered by Schreffler and Owen. Other genes of the same region are responsible for the capacity to stimulate "cellular immunity" in the recipient at the time of a graft. Cellular immunity refers to the attack on the graft by cells acting on the spot, as opposed to cells acting at a distance through the secretion of antibodies.

You need not retain all these details, except perhaps for the most surprising, the most unexpected discovery concerning this genetic area, namely, the discovery of immune response genes. This was a remarkable adventure in biology during recent years, and the tale is worth telling. Since all the facts are not in yet, I will spare you a detailed account of what we know so far. The following broad outline will be sufficient for the purposes of this book.

It had long been suspected that the reaction to a given infection differs from one individual to another. While one man suffering from an infectious disease dies, another recovers within a few days.

An Italian named Guido Biozzi, working in the laboratory of Bernard Halpern in Paris, was the first to demonstrate that the degree of defense reactions depended on heredity. He observed that in a mouse population the response to a series of infectious agents or foreign substances varied from one mouse to another. He selected those individuals with the weakest response and interbred them. Similarly, he interbred those with the strongest response. At the end of twenty mouse generations he had obtained two distinct strains, one where all the individuals responded strongly and the other where all responded poorly.

McDevitt in San Francisco and Benacerraf in Boston went further. They proved that certain immune response genes accounted for the response to a given agent, and to that agent alone. The result is that some animals respond well to one substance and poorly to another, whereas other animals may respond in the opposite way.

Everyone was astonished when it was found that many of these immune response genes are located in the very same chromosomal area as the H2 markers. In other words, the same minute region codes both the markers of our own individuality and our capacity to perceive and react against the markers of other individuals.

Susceptibility to Disease

Do men, like mice and guinea pigs, have individual differences in their susceptibility to various diseases? That was the next question. Is there any relationship between human HLA markers and the tendency to contract a particular disease, just as a relationship exists between H2 markers and immune response genes in the mouse? With the answer came an unexpected flood of information.

A man of fifty develops backache and discomfort on walking, and his doctor finds that his vertebrae and pelvis are invaded by a rheumatic disease called ankylosing spondylarthritis. His health has been perfect up to now. Yet from the very beginning of his life, this man has almost surely been predisposed to this disease, for most patients with this rheumatic illness (over 90 percent) carry the HLA marker labeled B27, which is found in only 5 percent of the rest of the population. Similarly, leprosy, allergy to pollens, psoriasis, myasthenia, and many other diseases appear to be related to certain HLA markers or pairs of HLA markers. The defense against the hepatitis B virus is stronger in individuals possessing HLA markers A1 and B8. We shall see later that similar relationships exist between the HLA markers and other illnesses, called the autoimmune diseases.

Allotypes and Idiotypes

The histocompatibility systems just discussed already afford immense possibilities of chemical variation among individuals of the same species. But other families of markers have been discovered which also distinguish individuals from each other. The work of Jacques Oudin and his co-workers in Paris in the 1950s is typical of these discoveries. As I have said before, our blood contains a family of large molecules which, following immunization, assume the role of antibodies. They are grouped together under the name of immunoglobulins, but they consist of many different classes and subclasses. At first blush, the classes and subclasses of immunoglobulins appear to be identical in all the animals of a particular species. Oudin discovered that this is not true, that, in fact, the molecular structure of one given class or subclass of immunoglobulins differs in some detail from one group of animals to another within the same species. Oudin demonstrated these differences in rabbits and called them allotypes. Very soon, similar differences were demonstrated in other species, including man, showing that the phenomenon discovered by Oudin is general.

For instance, one system of human immunoglobulin allotypes, named Gm by Grubb, working in Sweden, divides the human population into twenty-five groups. Another similar system, which may differ from one individual to the next, is called InV; it was discovered by Ropartz, working in Rouen. Since the Gm and InV systems are independent, and since several additional immunoglobulin allotype systems have been discovered in man, it is easy to see that the variety of possible combinations is infinite. Once more, we become aware of the uniqueness of the chemical makeup of each one of us, brought about through the interaction of innumerable hereditary markers.

Oudin also discovered another, more subtle difference between immunoglobulins of various individuals, and named it "idiotypic variation." An immunoglobulin which at first appears to be identical in two individuals, even belonging to the same allotype, may reveal differences *after these individuals have been immunized against a given substance.* These differences are called *idiotypes.* And to complicate matters even further, these idiotypes may vary not only from one individual to the next but also within the same individual from one immunizing substance to the next.

To be fair, however, one must mention that, in contrast with allotypes, the role of heredity in idiotypes has been clearly demonstrated only in a few cases in the rabbit and the mouse.

Of Horses and Oysters

The preceding illustrations will suffice, I believe, to convince the reader that in one given species each individual is different. Each individual inherits such a number of diverse chemical markers from his parents and ancestors that he cannot but be a unique chemical entity. Dozens of new articles concerning such genetic polymorphism are published each year in journals with such descriptive titles as *Animal Blood Groups and Biochemical Genetics, Genetics, Journal of Heredity, Heredity, Human Heredity, Journal de génétique humaine,* and so on. Whatever the animal studied, whatever the material studied, these articles all lead to remarkably similar conclusions. An investigator selects, almost at random, one or several molecules which make up an animal, for instance some of the innumerable enzymes which are the kernel of life. He analyzes them in a series of individuals belonging to an apparently homogenous group of animals. And three times out of four he finds individual differences, either in the fine structure or in the amount of the enzyme.

These differences exist throughout nature, in the human being as in animals. In a population of drosophila flies, for instance, two Chicago zoologists studied a series of points on the chromosomal map and demonstrated that 40 percent of them will generate molecules which differ significantly from one fly to the next. In London, Harris studied three enzymes in a series of British subjects and found that in an astonishing number of cases these three enzymes differ from one Briton to another, either in a small structural detail or by their degree of activity. And he proved that these differences follow the laws of heredity.

Similar observations have been made on the Australian trotting horse. On cattle. On pigeons and other birds. One oyster differs from the next within the variety called Ostrea edules. And the reading of the March 1974 issue of the *Journal of Genetics and Microbiology* reveals that a most simple germ, a Salmonella responsible for food poisoning, a perfectly well-defined microbial species, does not escape the same polymorphism.

So in all species, great and small, the individual finds a personal uniqueness in the variegated mixture of inherited material which he receives at birth from his ancestors and that he will in part transmit to his descendants.

Biological Immortality

Our children do not always resemble us as much as we would wish. They do not mirror their parents sufficiently to reconcile us with the idea of death. The rules of the game differ from what we would wish. For those of us who have had the good fortune to have children with a beloved husband or wife, we would no doubt simply ask that the qualities of the mother and the qualities of the father be joined in the children. It does not work that way. Certainly we give our children enough of the genes which have gone into the making of our own body for them to resemble us. But for other genes we play only the part of a passive messenger. We transmit genes to our children which were derived from our ancestors, but which played no role in fashioning our own person. We are only intermediaries, simple links in a network which emerges from the past and is directed, apparently at random, toward the future. Apparently at random, but we will come back later to what may be hidden behind these words.

Thus, little by little, the picture of our individual uniqueness is unveiled. Each of us is an original composition. The letters and words which make up our pages are not unique in themselves, each one may have belonged to millions of other individuals in the network in which we are but a link, but they have never before been assembled in the same manner. The probability is almost nil that the same assemblage of words and letters will someday reappear in exactly the same order—that in some fashion we might be reborn *in toto.* Yet it is less unlikely that others will inherit large parts of our physical individuality. Thus, each of us is mortal only as a whole, as a unique assembly. Has it ever happened to you, as it did to me once, to see your double? At a concert one evening I experienced a strange and sudden shock when I caught a glimpse of a musician who had my face. In any case, such a perpetuation of the material we are made of is the only form of immortality that biology can offer.

CHAPTER **Two**

In Defense of the Self

Not only is each person chemically unique, but each one possesses a remarkable system of surveillance to protect his uniqueness throughout life. This system is extremely complex and its details can be left to the specialist. But I would like to describe a few of its facets because they shed new light on the self and the non-self, or, if you prefer, the differences between one man and another and the way each man is linked to all of mankind.

The principles are simple. The mission of this internal system is to be on the lookout, at all times and in all places, for the individual markers which stamp the seal of our individuality on each element, each tissue of our body. If the seal is ours, the tissue is respected. If it is not, the tissue is attacked and destroyed.

The system of surveillance is composed of billions of specialized cells subdivided into a variety of classes. Each of these classes has its own role to play in the policing activity. Think of them as the sections of an orchestra, or the hierarchy in a society of bees, united in a complex organization working toward a common end.

Internal Surveillance

An artful device has been used to penetrate the microscopic world of these policing cells. A sample of these cells is taken from the blood and placed in an artificial medium which maintains life and even allows cells to grow. (The technical term is "cell culture.") It is then possible to subject these cells to careful study, in a model which is, of course, much simpler than the complex living body from which they came. These studies, performed in test tubes, are called *in vitro,* as opposed to *in vivo* studies, in the living body.

One of the most extensively used of such *in vitro* tests is the culture of lymphocytes. These are small, round cells of which there are about a thousand billion in our body, or two or three thousand in a cubic millimeter of blood. The study of lymphocyte culture has become so important that every year dozens of scientific meetings and congresses are devoted to that subject alone.

Those readers who are detective story fans know that unless they peek ahead they must wait for the end of the book to find out who the culprit is. In this book, however, I will present the lymphocytes without further ado. They are the No. 1 agent and the first element to react in the internal surveillance system which we are discussing.

Is it possible to study the reaction of the lymphocyte in the simplified *in vitro* system just described? When removed from the body, will the lymphocytes retain the same properties? Will the lymphocytes of Subject A be able to distinguish in the culture tube, as they do *in vivo,* the cells of Subject B from those of A—in other words, B markers from A markers? How will the lymphocytes behave?

The answers to all these questions turned out to be so surprisingly explicit that I was thrilled when I first observed the results under the microscope. It happened in the New York laboratory where Fritz Bach and Kurt Hirschhorn had made the discovery, at about the same time as did a young and shy Canadian, Barbara Bain.

The Mixed Lymphocyte Culture

Bach, Hirschhorn, and Bain use a very simple method to confront lymphocytes with a cell population taken from another individual: in the same medium, they mix and culture together two batches of lymphocytes, taken from two different subjects. This is called mixed lymphocyte culture. Soon afterwards, a number of the lymphocytes undergo a strange transformation. The little round cell, whose diameter measured not more than eight-thousandths of a millimeter at the start, has considerably enlarged. The round central nucleus, which earlier almost filled the cell, has doubled in size, and the rest of the cell has grown even more.

Simultaneously, the rate of proliferation of these lymphocytes is considerably accelerated. This is easily demonstrated by using the measurement of "labeled thymidine incorporation," a test which evaluates the production of DNA (deoxyribonucleic acid), located within the cell nucleus and involved in cell multiplication.

Further investigation showed that this transformation of lymphocytes does indeed result from the contact between cells coming from two different individuals, for it does not occur when the two lymphocyte populations come from the same individual.

This visible transformation of lymphocytes in the presence of foreign cells is the first in a chain of events which were soon uncovered. Lymphocyte transformation is rapidly followed by the appearance of certain lymphocytes which have acquired a killing potential. This power to kill is *specific,* directed only against the markers of the second population. In other words, if we designate the first lymphocyte population as *a,* taken from Individual A, and as *b* the second population, taken from Individual B, lymphocytes *a,* cultivated with lymphocytes *b,* can kill any cell from B but remain inoffensive toward cells from other individuals unless these individuals have some markers in common with B.

The attack of killing lymphocytes is accompanied by the release of a variety of substances called "mediators," or "lymphokins," which participate in the attack. Some of these mediators summon auxiliary cells, macrophages, to the rescue. The macrophages are attracted, held to the spot, and endowed with a blind capacity of killing all undesirable cells within reach.

A large part of what I have just described has been demonstrated in rather artificial *in vitro* conditions. But other investigations—including some to which my own research group has devoted a lot of time—have shown that similar events also take place *in vivo,* within the living being. For instance, the lymphocytes of a kidney transplant recipient undergo the same singular transformation just described in the *in vitro* mixed lymphocyte culture. To a large extent the *in vitro* tests illustrate the successive events which in the body lead to the phenomenon of graft rejection.

However, as frequently happens in the history of science, reality soon turned out to be far more complex than this first approach suggested.

Superintendents and Specialists

The simple scheme of three successive events by which the lymphocytes first recognize the graft as alien, then are transformed, and finally become capable of killing the graft was but a first step on the road. Soon it became evident that while all lymphocytes resemble each other at first glance, they include in fact a series of different populations which differ vastly from each other in their function and in the place they occupy in the organization of the defense system. The scheme which I am about to outline will illustrate the surprising specialization of each one of these populations and the surprising way in which they coordinate their action.

The principal function of certain lymphocytes is to register and to record in their own data bank a message concerning the molecular disposition of alien markers. This message is transmitted to other lymphocytes. Among these, some are destined to become the killers of every element bearing these alien markers. Others are remarkable for their ability to undergo the extraordinary transformation earlier described and to foster the development of aggressive cells. Still others operate quite differently. They manufacture circulating antibodies that will attach themselves to their prey and render it extremely vulnerable to the action of a chemical system within us called Complement, a system always ready to attack when triggered by certain "activators." Other antibodies can render their prey vulnerable not to Complement but to certain normal cells such as those sometimes called the K cells. The role of still other lymphocytes, called "suppressors," is to moderate and regulate the intensity of the various aggressive mechanisms. These suppressor lymphocytes are perhaps the conductors of the orchestra formed by all the specialized populations, according their efforts toward a common goal, the defense of individuality.

Many of these effects can bring about what may be called countereffects. For instance, certain antibodies directed against a given prey can block the aggressivity of the lymphocytes directed against this prey.

From all this, one can easily imagine the multiform and coordinated world which constitutes the army responsible for the defense of our chemical personality and the repelling of any foreign invasion. One question immediately comes to mind. Why does such a powerful army, so prompt to react and attack, remain inoffensive toward our own body? What is the secret of the pacific coexistence between our own tissues, diverse and innumerable as they are, and our own lymphocytes and other killing agents?

Respect of the Self

About 1940 a group at the London Mill Hill Institute of Research thought that they had discovered the secret of the tolerance which our body enjoys in the face of the menacing army it harbors. The findings of the British investigators were so clear and so convincing that the leader of the team, Sir Peter Medawar, was awarded the Nobel Prize for his remarkable work. He observed that if cells from animal B were introduced into animal A in the hours preceding birth, animal A would then become tolerant to all tissues coming from animal B. It was reasonable to conclude that before birth the body's defense agents make an inventory of all the markers within an individual (including the alien markers fraudulently introduced in the experiment described above) and that the body then acquires a definitive tolerance for all these markers. Thereafter, the integrity of the person is respected as it was constituted, chemically speaking, on the day of his birth.

Unfortunately, this simple and attractive interpretation leaves certain questions unanswered. We still know very little about what is behind this tolerance of the self. What is its secret mechanism? How are lymphocytes modified to make them able to preserve our integrity but to attack invaders? Lymphocytes live but a few weeks; how do they transmit all this information to their successors?

Imaginative minds have built up the most fantastic hypotheses to explain this mechanism. Of course, even the most careful biologist is free to dream. But his dreams have no final value until concrete projects verify whether they should be pursued or lead only to a dead end. This is the very principle of modern science. More than a century ago the French physiologist Claude Bernard pointed out in his *Introduction à la médecine expérimentale* that the imagination of scientists should not merely build theories but rather inspire experiments capable of answering Yes or No to the initial speculation.

At the present moment the dreams inspired by the problem of the recognition of self (their authors call them "theories") are still too imprecise to explain with certainty how our defense agents learn to respect our body. One fact is certain, surprising though it may be: within the reactions of these defense agents, there is no clear-cut separation between tolerance and aggressivity. Between these two opposite responses, the line of demarcation is thin. A classic experiment by Mitchison will illustrate the point. If one milligram of bovine serum albumin is injected into a mouse, the animal will undergo immunization and will manufacture antibodies against this substance. If a smaller amount is injected—one-tenth of a milligram—not only will the mouse not be immunized but it will become tolerant, that is, it becomes unable to manufacture antibodies even if the same substance is later injected in a dose which would be sufficient to produce immunity in a normal mouse.

This fact has been confirmed through many similar experiments, for instance through those performed by Ada and Parish in the institute directed by Gus Nossal in Melbourne. One given substance, depending upon the dosage, can be equally immunogenic—that is, able to produce immunity—or tolerogenic—that is, able to prevent immunization of the animal by this substance. Let me add that the same dose may be immunogenic or tolerogenic depending upon whether it is injected through the skin or directly into the veins.

Breakdown in the Respect of Self: Autoimmune Disease

Knowing that these two apparently opposed reactions, tolerance and immunity, are not as far from each other as it might seem will prepare the reader to be less surprised by the following phenomenon. It sometimes happens that the tolerance which our immune system accords our own body breaks down. The army within our body will then attack our own tissues as if they were alien. This pathological disorder is termed an "autoimmune phenomenon," immunity against ourselves.

The number of diseases where such phenomena are suspected is now considerable. Among other examples, let me cite multiple sclerosis, certain forms of nephritis, certain anemias, certain diseases of the lung, the eye, and the skin. Rather than go into detail concerning each one of these diseases, I will choose one which in everybody's mind is particularly characteristic of autoimmune disease.

This disease goes by the somewhat complicated name of disseminated lupus erythematosus and is commonly referred to as lupus. It primarily affects young women and manifests itself by pain in the joints, fever, and involvement of various tissues and organs—skin, kidney, liver, and others. Simultaneously, antibodies against certain chemical structures of our own body appear in the blood, for instance against deoxyribonucleic acid (DNA), an intranuclear material which carries our hereditary code.

The tendency to manufacture autoantibodies is one of the characteristic features of this disease. This propensity is part of a complex imbalance in the immunological response, which becomes insufficient in some areas, blind and excessive in others. An illness very similar to human disseminated lupus is found in certain mice. Many investigators see in this mouse disease a model of the human disease, and they hope that the study of mice will reveal the secrets of the innermost mechanisms in disseminated lupus. Only particular species of mice are affected—especially the New Zealand mice labeled NZB and NZB/NZW. These mice develop antibodies, notably against DNA, and die prematurely with all the signs and symptoms of an autoimmune disease injuring many organs, such as the kidney.

It has been possible to study the immunological disorder which appears to be the primary cause of disease in these mice. J. F. Bach in our laboratory in Paris demonstrated that the secretion from the thymus gland drops at a very early age in these mice. It so happens that the thymus plays a major role in the normal maturation of the defense system. Jacques Miller, a native of Nice working primarily in London and later in Melbourne, showed years ago that animals deprived of thymus at birth lose a large part of their power to reject grafts. This means that the recognition of alien tissues is greatly influenced by the thymus. In fact, this gland is responsible for the "maturation" of lymphocytes in charge of surveillance of the self and endows them with the qualities necessary for the accomplishment of this task.

Now, like the NZB mouse, women suffering from lupus have a less active thymus than do healthy women of the same age. Imaginative investigators quickly seized upon these findings to explain lupus. This illness could result from an anomaly in the thymus gland arising out of a failure in the hereditary chain of command which presides over the life of the thymus, its development, and the timing of its slow and progressive decline which takes place in everyone during the course of his life. Another possibility would be that the defect of the thymus could be caused by the invasion of an unknown virus.

The thymus, as I have already said, is largely responsible for maintaining the equilibrium which normally reigns in the complicated little world of our immunological defenses. It delivers into the circulation an agent, a hormone, which regulates the life of certain categories of lymphocytes, particularly the "suppressing" lymphocytes which control the manufacture of antibodies. Consequently, it is not surprising that the immunological disorders of lupus may be the consequence of a poorly active thymus. This kind of explanation is all the more provocative since the product secreted by the thymus and insuring the maturation of the lymphocytes is now known, can be manufactured, and will soon be in the hands of the physician. The deficiency of many glands, the thyroid and the adrenal for instance, has been overcome through the substitution of manufactured hormones. There is a possibility that the same method may be applicable to patients with faulty thymus activity.

You can easily understand that the study of autoimmune

disease provides a useful tool in our attempt to comprehend mechanisms which normally protect us from autoimmunity, or—to put it differently—to protect our body from attacks from within. But, notwithstanding the progress which I have just cited, the innermost mechanism responsible for the respect of the self remains, I repeat, full of mystery.

We will come back to this system of defense a little later when it will become necessary to place it in the framework of another, larger enigma: Is the fierce immunologic defense of individuality significant in the evolution of man through the ages?

CHAPTER Three

Human Diversity:
The Key to Survival

The life span of molecules, the stuff that cells are made of, is ephemeral. The cells which constitute our bodies vanish at regular intervals, to be replaced by others. Our body itself is destined to die. And we now know that living species also are mortal. Some 50 percent of the animal species that have existed on the earth have disappeared today.

So far, we have but a small insight into the rules that govern the strange game of life and death of species. What we know about the subject is most clearly stated in the book entitled *On the Origin of Species by Means of Natural Selection,* written by the English naturalist Charles Darwin in 1859.

Up to that time no one had succeeded in challenging the

idea that all living species had been created once and for all, and that each of them was forever immutable. To be fair, the concept of the fixity of species had been subjected to critical examination by a few writers during the eighteenth century. In 1748, Benoit de Maillet published *Entretiens d'un philosophe indien avec un missionnaire français sur la diminution de la mer* (Conversations of an Indian Philosopher and a French Missionary on the Receding of the Sea). In this essay he suggests that certain marine animals developed first out of primitive germs, which he calls "seeds." Later, adapting to different environments, some of these creatures underwent transformations which allowed them to move to the land or to take wing. "We would find," de Maillet goes on to say, "the transformation of fish into birds far more difficult to believe did we not witness the metamorphosis of a silkworm or of a caterpillar into a butterfly. The 'seeds' or spawn of these same fish could have been responsible for an initial transmigration of the species from sea to land. Had one hundred million individuals died during this endeavor, the success of one pair would have been sufficient to create the new species."

But de Maillet's ideas were lost in such a hodgepodge of vanishing suns, soaring whirlwinds, and rushing deluges that everyone, from Voltaire to Flourens, only laughed.

In 1768, René Robinet published an essay, "Nature Learning to Create Man," where, long before Teilhard de Chardin, he suggested the idea that through the successive transformations of existing creatures, nature moves forward progressively in search of perfection. "Man," he writes, "is the masterpiece of nature, but aiming for perfection, nature could not reach it except through a series of innumerable trials. . . . Each variation of a prototype is a kind of study for the human form over which nature is pondering."

But the great Buffon himself, in his *Natural History,* maintained that he could reduce to naught the idea of the evolution of the species. Only at the end of his life did he admit: "The form of animals is not unalterable. Their nature can change completely with time. The more delicate, the heavier, the less active, the less well-armed, etc., have already disappeared or will disappear." This is nothing less than an early expression of the concept of natural selection.

It was Lamarck who took the idea one step further in his *Zoological Philosophy,* published in 1809. But his explanation of the process of evolution was naive. "The species," he explained, "can become transformed in time as a response to external circumstances." "The mole," he continued, "has no eyes because it always lives underground; bats have acquired wings because they had the habit of jumping; snakes have smooth bodies because they slither through narrow passages; the giraffe has an excessively long neck because it must stretch it continuously to reach the foliage in high trees."*

"This is the silliest, most superficial idea," commented the great naturalist Cuvier some years later. "Bodies are somehow thought to be molded by hand, put together like lumps of dough or clay. He who dares to suggest seriously that a fish, by staying out of water, could see his scales eventually turn into feathers, only displays the most profound ignorance of anatomy."

But Saint-Hilaire, another naturalist, no less famous, con-

---

*This is not a full quotation. I have chosen significant parts only.

sidered this banter simplistic and declared, "Obviously, imperceptible change is not the means by which lower types of animals have achieved a higher degree of organization." This was the first suggestion that sudden deep *mutations* could explain the transformation of one species into another, without any known intermediary steps.

At last came Darwin. The heated controversies of preceding centuries had gradually prepared the way, as frequently happens for those who are fortunate enough to make important discoveries when the time is ripe for their acceptance.

Darwin started from an observation which can easily be verified because we see it happening every day right before our eyes. He called it variation under domestication—in other words, artificial selection by man. How have growers succeeded in breeding animals and plants which serve their needs? They have chosen the best varieties of fruit trees, grains, vegetables, or flowers, and neglected or destroyed the others. They have crossed animals to breed a special characteristic which appealed to them. And within a few generations they have obtained from these apparently accidental varieties new breeds where all individuals exhibit this characteristic. In the same way they have learned how to transform the slate-blue wild rock pigeon into pigeons with multicolored breasts, or fantails, or carrier pigeons. For hunting they have kept only the dogs who were good pointers or retrievers.

According to Darwin's theory, nature has been able to do the same thing. Natural selection was a necessity for beings to adapt in a hostile world. This is what Herbert Spencer called "the survival of the fittest." And changes produced by natural selection can be much more profound than those produced by the breeder, because nature can count on millions of years, while the breeder has at his disposal only the ridiculously short span of his own life.

The Birth of Genetics

In the years following Darwin's theory, several important discoveries were to provide a golden key to all future discussions. Various possible mechanisms were uncovered which could explain the transformation of a living being. The understanding of these mechanisms came with immense progress in genetics, the science of heredity.

In the first part of this book we alluded to the manner in which heredity depends essentially, although not exclusively, on genes residing within the chromosomal material found in the cell nuclei. Each parent transmits one-half of his genes to the child and, as genes determine the child's makeup, the biological individuality of the child will depend on the chance encounter between maternal and paternal genes. Chance, indeed, but chance governed by such rigid rules that if one forgets the individual and considers the species as a whole, the basic material of heredity appears fixed, constant, and characteristic of a specific group such as the human species. Chance enters only into the distribution of this hereditary material among individuals.

Yet the idea that the hereditary material in a living species is stable is only a first approach. In reality, this material is subject to many variations. Some of them appear almost accidental, for example a mutation—a sudden change in the chemical composition of a gene, or the loss or acquisition of fragments of the hereditary material on the chromosome map. So much has been said about these mutations apropos of their dangerous increase after atomic radiation that the reader is probably familiar with this phenomenon.

Let us take a concrete example from the work of Linus Pauling. Hemoglobin, the pigment responsible for the red color of blood, has the structure of a long molecular chain made of a series of links, one of which is glutamic acid. The manufacture of this acid is programmed, "coded," in the hereditary material by a "codon" made up of a trio named GAG. (GAG stands for the purine bases guanine, adenine, guanine.) But a mutation can occur inducing the replacement of the middle substance, adenine, by uracil: GAG then becomes GUG. GUG determines the manufacture, not of glutamic acid, but of another substance, valine, which then takes the place of the usual glutamic acid in the structure of hemoglobin. Individuals who inherit the gene for this modified hemoglobin will suffer from a disease which is widespread in Africa, called drepanocytosis, or sickle-cell anemia. This last label suggests the sickle shape which these abnormal red cells take as soon as the slightest lack of oxygen occurs. Later we will see how the mutation of the hemoglobin works in human selection by creating, on the one hand, a weakness at times fatal and, on the other, an unexpected defense against certain outside agents.

Mutations, Migrations, and Drifting

There are still other mechanisms to explain the evolution of the species over the course of time. For instance, drifting, where a gene is not modified but its frequency increases or decreases from generation to generation. Similar phenomena may occur, for example, when the migration of populations to other climes results in geographic isolation. This interferes with the laws of chance by limiting the diversity possible in the mixture of hereditary characteristics.

It is not my purpose, nor am I competent, to take part in the very lively discussions among those who, over the last century, have sought to understand the evolution of living beings. The simple idea that this evolution can be explained entirely by natural selection operating on the basis of chance—that is, mutations, migration, and drifts, as well as other modifying influences—is under heavy attack today. It seems to me that the discussion becomes clearer if we consider separately two quite distinct problems.

First: Are living species derived from each other? Is man descended from the monkey? Can one explain the birth of each new species through known or likely mechanisms of evolution? I believe that, contrary to appearances, this first question is far from being completely answered, contrary to what was hoped a few years ago. Therefore we will leave it aside, for it matters little in our present discussion.

Second: (This is the question that does matter in our analysis, and luckily we can consider it resolved.) Within a given species—the fly, the mouse, or man—do selective phenomena take place? The answer to this question is almost unanimously in the affirmative. Selection can result in the evolution of the species, adapt it to outside conditions, assure its survival in a hostile world, or, on the contrary, threaten its survival and bring about its disappearance. To illustrate these points, I will cite three examples, two taken from animals, one from man.

The Resistance of Germs to Antibiotics

When the first antibiotics were discovered, everyone thought that no germs would be able to resist them. This would be the end of infectious diseases. Those known to be 100 percent fatal, like subacute bacterial endocarditis or tuberculous meningitis, were miraculously cured by the new drugs. They were so powerful that germs did not have a chance to resist. As the use of antibiotics spread throughout the world, one was led to expect that the germs which are the most dangerous to man would simply disappear under this fierce bombardment.

But before long the unexpected occurred: not only did the microorganisms under attack not disappear, but they acquired a resistance to the antibiotic which but a short time before did them in with such ease. Other antibiotics had to be used against the germs resistant to the initial one. But the cycle repeated itself. Each time a new agent was discovered —apparently all-powerful at first—little by little the number of germs able to resist it increased.

Here is one example out of many. In 1963, Weinstein developed a new extract from a microscopic mushroom of the genus Microspora. This product is called gentamicin. It proved to be active against many kinds of germs. For instance, Pseudomonas aeruginosa, the bacillus of blue pus which is so difficult to destroy, yielded to the new medication in every case. Janine Witchitz and Y. Chabert in the *Journal of Antibiotics* published the first case of resistance to gentamicin; this was in 1969. Five years later Witchitz reported that 31.03 percent of the same germ that she had examined over the five preceding months were resistant to gentamicin. This seems to me a perfect example of how a living species confronted with apparently death-dealing outside conditions is able to survive and to adapt itself to adverse situations. But what is the mechanism of this adaptation?

At first one might think that the germ defends itself through transformations induced by the antibiotic. Indeed, if such a mechanism exists, it is the exception, not the rule. The rule is very different, as the work done in the laboratories of Luria and Lederberg shows. (These two scientists were rewarded by the Nobel Prize in 1969 and 1958, respectively.)* The secret of this resistance is as follows: While the germs may all look alike, this appearance masks a crucial diversity. The population which comes in contact with the antibiotic does not consist of perfectly identical individuals. Given a million germs of the genus Pseudomonas aeruginosa, for instance, the structure and the molecular composition of the great majority are such as to allow their

---

*Originally this research was not to study bacterial resistance to antibiotics, but to other enemies of bacteria, namely, bacteriophages. But this does not alter the point.

destruction by gentamicin; but a few of them differ from the others, precisely at one of the vulnerable points. This vulnerable point may vary from one antibiotic to another,* but in the mass of sensitive microorganisms there will usually be a few individuals who do not have this weak point and are therefore invulnerable. These resistant individuals will be able to grow in spite of the antibiotic. They will give birth to new generations which will differ from the former by their resistance to the antibiotic, and this will save the species. Thus the antibiotic will have effected not a direct transformation of the living species, but a selection of individuals able to weather the storm, and who will be a starting point for the survival of the species. In brief, if the species does not die, it is because it is not uniform, because chemical differences—"mutations," to use the proper term—are hidden behind the apparently identical appearance of all the germs.

These mutations are such an integral and essential part of the life of a species that, even in the case of living creatures so small and relatively simple as germs, they are organized according to a characteristic rhythm which we are beginning to perceive and to analyze. It goes by the intriguing name of "periodic selection."

*Germs have a number of points at which they can be vulnerable to antibiotics. Examples are: the cell surface membrane (permeable to the antibiotic except in resistant individuals), or the lack of an enzyme capable of destroying the antibiotic (versus the presence of such an enzyme in resistant bacteria). Another mechanism may be that the antibiotic so closely resembles a material necessary for bacterial life that it deceives the bacteria, takes the place of the vital material, and in a manner "starves" the bacteria; in resistant germs the resemblance is less and the scheme fails.

I have purposely simplified the facts—the whole truth is more complex. For instance, we know today that, in the case of microorganisms such as the Pseudomonas aeruginosa, the molecules on which resistance depends are found not only in the principal hereditary code situated in the nucleus of the living cell, but also in little fragments of separate, naked coding material named plasmids by Lederberg. A remarkable fact about these plasmids is that they are infectious; they can penetrate neighboring germs. That is, a microorganism, bearer of a plasmid responsible for resistance to an antibiotic, not only protects itself but also communicates the secret of its invulnerability to numerous other germs of its species. But these superimposed mechanisms involved in species survival should not obscure the basic ideas outlined above: if all individuals were identical, their community could easily be obliterated.

Resistance of Insects to Insecticides

Creating a chemical environment hostile to insects may be another interesting model for studying the way species react' to hostile environments in order to survive.

While dichloro-diphenyl-trichloro-ethane (generally called DDT) is the best known, insecticides number in the thousands today. In the United States alone there are 58,831 different brands of pesticides for combating insects and other animals inimical to man and to his crops.

Insects are among the most ferocious enemies of man. A mosquito, the female Anopheles, is the agent transmitting malaria. Before the era of pesticides, malaria killed five million persons every year. Today the use of insecticides has reduced this mortality by 80 percent. In India, for example, the incidence of malaria has been reduced by a factor of fifteen, and life expectancy has increased by fifteen years. In his book *Before Nature Dies,* Professor Jean Dorst tells of the terrible epidemic of malaria which followed the accidental importation of a few Anopheles into the Brazilian province of Natal by a French ship coming from Dakar. This incident remains a painful memory in the minds of Brazilians. The mosquito soon quit the city of Natal, but migrated northward and in 1938 spread a terrible epidemic of malaria in Rio Grande do Norte and Ceará. To quote the Brazilian writer Sampaio: "The mosquitoes advanced like hordes of bloodthirsty Huns leaving a train of death and destruction in their wake." There were hundreds of thousands of cases of malaria and more than 20,000 deaths. Two years later insecticides had conquered the Anopheles and the disease had disappeared.

Another point: at a time when famine stalks the earth, insects are formidable competitors for the world's food supply. It has been estimated that every year insects devour enough to feed 40 million men. Hence, humanity owes a lot to insecticides.

But here again, just as with germs and antibiotics, insects did not give up so easily when faced with insecticides. As early as 1945 a dozen species which had become resistant to insecticides had been identified and listed. In 1946 a report from Sweden called attention to the fact that Swedish flies were beginning to resist DDT. In 1947 Italian mosquitoes refused to succumb to this insecticide. In 1949 the Greek Anopheles joined the resistance movement. The red spider, which attacks forage and crop plants, provides a worldwide example of the race between the search for new pesticides and the unrelenting development of resistance. There are today more than 350 species of insects which have become resistant to dozens of different insecticides.

Multiple mechanisms probably account for this deep-seated resistance. Recent studies suggest that insects have more than one trick in their genetic kit to save their species from annihilation.* But the fundamental principle is the same as the one operating in the resistance of germs to antibiotics: insect populations which appear to be identical when viewed as a whole turn out to include individuals sufficiently different in structural details for the toxic product to "select" the few creatures able to resist, kill the others, and make it possible for the succeeding generations

---

*In order to illustrate the complexity of these phenomena, which I have presented in simplified form, I will mention the studies made by Ramade and Beard. They showed that a weak dose of insecticides can operate through a mechanism different from selection. This was demonstrated by the following observation. In 1952 farmers on an agricultural cooperative near Paris noticed that the insecticides with which they were coating the stables and sheepfolds no longer killed the flies. A sample of these flies was sent to Ramade, who verified that this was true. He kept and bred these flies through 186 successive generations in his laboratory. Painting the cages with the insecticide lindane increased the resistance of the insects without apparent selection, since none were killed. The resistance diminished by degrees when the painting of the cages with insecticide was stopped. This resembles the phenomenon called mithridatism, in memory of King Mithridates, who tried to become invulnerable to poisons by regularly swallowing small doses. I shall not enter into the molecular mechanisms which were put forward to explain these facts—they interest the specialist. These complementary mechanisms should not cloud the basic role of selection. And it may be relevant to mention that, according to Ramade, the proportion of insects who may be spontaneously resistant to an insecticide is commonly less than 5 in 1,000.

to be composed of descendants of the few survivors, who can transmit to these new generations the characteristics responsible for this resistance. Like the phoenix rising from its ashes, a renewed species resistant to the deadly agent is born again. The species, germ or mosquito, would have been threatened with extinction had all individuals been identical. Genetic polymorphism appears to be an indispensable element to insure survival in hard times.

Resistance to Malaria in Men Carrying the Gene of Sickle-Cell Anemia

In the 1950s physicians working in Africa made an observation which provides an interesting model for those who would reflect on the subtleties of the game of life and death of human populations.

Africa is one of the continents where the parasite of malaria is prevalent. It is the region of the world where the most virulent variety of this parasite prevails, the death-dealing Plasmodium falciparum. Sickle-cell anemia, the result of a hereditary anomaly of the blood cells, is also largely an African disease.

As you will recall, sickle-cell anemia owes its name to the fact that when the oxygen content of the blood is even slightly reduced in individuals who have inherited this anomaly, their red blood cells lose their spherical shape and take on a crescent form resembling a sickle. This induces a certain degree of anemia. In some regions, from the Sahel to Zambia, up to 40 percent of black Africans are affected by this anomaly. Fortunately, there are many benign and even latent forms of sickle-cell anemia. They do not threaten life, but the patients transmit the anomaly to future generations. In the more severe cases, children and adolescents may die from acute anemia, blood clots, heart failure, or progressive renal failure. The other side of the coin, however, is that blacks with this abnormal hemoglobin have an increased resistance to malaria and to its consequences. A study published in the *British Medical Journal* in 1954 showed that, among blacks living in Kenya and the Sudan, malaria is 38.4 percent less frequent in individuals with abnormal hemoglobin than it is in the rest of the population. And when, in spite of their natural resistance, individuals with sickle cells do contract malaria, they have benign forms with few malarial parasites invading their blood.

Since the parasite must spend part of its life inside red blood cells, the greater resistance of these individuals to malaria may be precisely due to their abnormal blood cells. The parasite probably finds penetration into these cells more difficult than into normal cells. Some suggest that there is an anomaly of the cell membrane associated with the anomaly of the hemoglobin pigment—the exact nature of this mechanism is not yet clear.

In any case, the essential point is that the situation can be depicted as an equilibrium between two kinds of risk: the risk of death through the hereditary blood disease, and the risk of death from malaria.

Considering this equilibrium a little more closely, we come to an unexpected conclusion: the noxious outside agent represented by malaria encourages the development of abnormal hemoglobin in the population at risk, thus modifying the evolution of the species.

This fact can be both proved and explained. The proof: among blacks in the United States, where there is no malaria, not only is the number of individuals with abnormal hemoglobin far smaller (less than 10 percent) than in countries infested with malaria, but, according to most observers, this abnormality is in the process of dying out. The explanation: just as among insects insecticides increase the proportion of individuals capable of resistance, malaria introduces a selective advantage—from generation to generation the number of individuals with the abnormal hemoglobin increases, simply because the others are decimated by malaria and have fewer descendants. It is easy to see how a superficial observer could believe, wrongly, that the hereditary abnormal hemoglobin is a phenomenon of adaptation in the human species, secondary to the aggression by the parasite. This reasoning would be wrong, as is so often the case when the final outcome is taken as an explanation. In fact, the parasite does not modify individuals, it only juggles with the existing variations among them, selecting some in favor of others. But it is clear that in the course of centuries such a selection disturbs the equilibrium between what we could call the different chemical varieties of man. It consequently leads to an evolution, a slow transformation, of the whole, which we call the human species.

Advantages and Disadvantages Bestowed by Heredity

The preceding example shows how difficult it may be to qualify a single hereditary characteristic as advantageous or disadvantageous, and consequently to evaluate the chances that this characteristic will develop or, on the contrary, regress in the course of human evolution.

It is a *disadvantage* to have the sickle-cell disease because this disease can be fatal in infancy. But it is an *advantage* insofar as it protects against the lethal dangers of malaria, and we have seen that this protection tends to favor the progression of the hereditary taint in the species.

Actually, there are many individual variations where neither advantage nor disadvantage is apparent. This frequently goes by the technical name of *neutral polymorphism,* meaning, for instance, that a particular variation in a body enzyme does not produce a selective effect from generation to generation and therefore does not influence the evolution of the species. There is no known advantage or disadvantage, for example, in having blue eyes as opposed to brown.

Similarly, one can ask what advantages or disadvantages may arise from the immune response genes, whose importance I discussed in the first part of this book. On May 8, 1972, thirty-eight specialists on this problem met in Augusta, Michigan. Some of them reported findings like those of Guido Biozzi in Paris, that the response against a family of germs called Salmonella is more forceful in some breeds of mice than in others; but the mice who manufacture a greater amount of antibodies against the markers of these germs are paradoxically far less well protected against these same germs than are those who do not have this beautiful reaction. The former cannot even be vaccinated, while the vaccine, which induces preventive immunization, easily protects the latter, who by heredity are but feebly responsive and manufacture very few antibodies. This is indeed a strange paradox, and its detailed explanation cannot be discussed here. It is enough to say that a large amount of antibodies can block certain defense mechanisms, and also that the hereditary characteristics just mentioned are linked with alterations in a special type of cells involved in the immune response and called macrophages. Let me give you another example. New Zealand mice, which we discussed earlier in Chapter 2, manufacture antibodies much more easily than do some other mice such as those labeled DBA or DBA/2. These latter mice usually lead a normal, healthy life, while the New Zealand mice, who apparently have the wherewithal to defend themselves so well against foreign substances, die prematurely from an illness in which they attack their own tissue, an autoimmune disease.

This kind of study is just beginning in man, but the first observations are sufficiently suggestive for one of the participants in the Michigan conference to feel that he could commit himself to the following conclusion: "As a geneticist I agree with Voltaire's Candide that 'this is the best of all possible worlds.' I still believe in Darwinian selection and I think that genetic systems in a wild population, under natural conditions, are the best of all possible collections of genes, taking into account the past history of any group." He went on to say, in substance, that apart from obviously lethal genes (and even these may be of some advantage for the population as a whole, as with the sickle-cell disease in a malarial environment), it was impossible for him to say whether a gene is bad or good. Thus, in the case of immune response genes, one individual may not have enough to maintain an effective surveillance of his self and will die of cancer, while another may have too many and will die of an autoimmune disease. He went on to say that possessing a gene such as that which protects against malarial parasites might be paid for with lower protection against some other aggressions such as cancer-promoting viruses.

I am inclined to think that we are not yet in a position to adopt so definite a conclusion. We must wait for additional research before the subject becomes entirely clear. But what is already certain is that the evolution of species, including the human species, is based on the diversity of individuals, a diversity maintained through well-established natural mechanisms. If this diversity did not exist, the species would probably be fated to extinction.

Here we see the most recent biological findings joining the age-old taboo forbidding incest. There would be a great risk for the human species if every individual did not receive from an unrelated father and mother a sufficiently varied collection of genes to insure his individuality in respect to other men.

CHAPTER *Four*

The Riddle of the Brain

The heart, the lung, the liver, and the kidney of a small animal are just as admirably and efficiently organized and refined in their function as they are in man. This is true, I believe, for all organs, for all tissues, for all cells. With, however, one exception—an exception that makes man different from any animal, including the larger monkeys. I am referring to the brain, man's truly unique feature.

The brain of man is usually considered to be the structure supporting his intellectual activity, and its remarkable development to parallel the development of language. The American philosopher Noam Chomsky has written: "As far as we know, possession of human language is associated with a specific type of mental organization, not simply a higher degree of intelligence. There seems to be no substance to the view that human language is simply a more complex instance of something to be found elsewhere in the animal world." Charles Darwin himself, who did so much in his *Descent of Man* to demonstrate some continuity between animal and human mental mechanisms, emphasized the difference separating human and animal brain activity— at least in magnitude. This remarkable development of the brain in man is reflected in his mastery over all other creatures. The American author of *The Ascent of Man,* Jacob Bronowski, writes: "The horse and the rider have many anatomical features in common. But it is the human creature that rides the horse, and not the other way about."

It is not surprising that physicians and biologists give special attention to the brain. The physician, when the time comes to define the end point of life—the limit beyond which any more treatment would be unacceptable obstinacy outside the true medical mission—accepts the total death of the brain as convincing evidence that the patient is no longer a living person. The physician's aim is not to prolong artificially the life of a few organs but rather to defend the life of the human person as a whole, and there is no longer a human person when the last spark of thought has been extinguished.

For the biologist, it is no less crucial to know whether the laws of biology apply to the brain as they do to other organs —in other words, whether his discoveries are applicable only to the body or are of interest to the whole man, body and soul. Even if the task is somewhat frightening, we must discuss whether the new data on the game of life should also be taken into account when studying the human mind.

The subject is awesome indeed. As soon as we approach the frontier between the body and the soul, between the brain and the mind, we are moved by a singular emotion. All our deepest convictions come to the fore. Passions enter into the discussion. And still if I believed, as Pascal said, that "We are made up of two opposed natures, the soul and the body," if I believed that my soul, like my body, were given to me by an all-powerful creator, I do not see what could be disrespectful or shocking in the thought that my brain might be the instrument chosen by God to give me a soul.

However, to respect everyone's feelings, I will try to present first an over-all view of concrete biological data on which everyone can agree regardless of personal beliefs. Only later will I venture to extend my reflections into the no man's land where men are no longer in accord.

Analogies between the System of Immunity and the Nervous System

During the last few years great progress has been made in the study of the brain. Little by little we are penetrating the mysteries. We are beginning to understand how external stimuli produce signals which will be suitably coded by the neurons, the cells of the nervous system, and how the signals are then transmitted to centers where the information is handled appropriately.

And today we are going even further. We are applying to the study of the brain the modern methods of cell biology, in an attempt to reach its innermost molecular mechanisms. Although I am not a specialist in neurobiology, I believe that in the study of the neurons we are seeing the beginning of a great adventure, similar to the adventure of immunology in which I have been engaged in my own research.

Many immunologists have been struck by this analogy. Niels Kaj Jerne, a Dane, director of a large institute for immunological research in Switzerland, concluded a speech at the Pasteur Institute in Paris in 1973 by saying, "I should like to point out that the immune system bears a striking resemblance to the nervous system. These two systems stand out among all other organs of our body by their ability to respond adequately to an enormous variety of signals."

"The number of nerve cells, like the number of immunological cells, is infinite," Dr. Jerne continued in substance. "Both have the capacity to recognize foreign signals, to react, and to adapt to the outside world. Both systems learn from experience and build up a memory, and that which is imprinted early in life is most deeply engraved."

Later I will go on to the conclusion of this speech, but first let me mention that the nervous system, intricate though it be, appears to be a symmetrical and harmonious architectural arrangement of billions of neurons. The properties of these cells are amazing. Their number alone (and, even more, the number of connections between them) strains our comprehension. In just the cortex, the bark of the brain, there are said to be ten thousand million neurons and one hundred thousand billion connections (called synapses) between neurons. Some investigators believe that these figures are understated. According to these calculations, the number of synapses under one man's skull is 30,000 times greater than the entire population of the globe. There is no comparison between this number and the number of elements in the most sophisticated tool constructed by man, the computer, where the number of connections hardly exceeds a million.*

The brain cells, like all the other cells in the body, manufacture protein molecules. They even produce these molecules at a rate which is among the most rapid in the human body. The life of each of these molecules is brief—a few minutes, a few hours, or a few days (the average "life" of 90 percent of these molecules is fourteen days). When a protein molecule disappears, it is immediately replaced by a fresh one, probably identical with the first, a perpetual motion which defies the imagination.

A computer not only has many fewer connections than does the nervous system, but its juxtaposed elements are identical. In the nervous system, on the contrary, there is an incredible diversity among the neurons. An example proving this was provided by Roger Sperry, working in Chicago in the 1940s. He performed the following experiment, which may shock sensitive people, but demonstrated the astonishing fact that a neuron can *recognize* the neuron with

*Here are the technical details, which I owe to the courtesy of Professors J. L. Lions and E. Gelende, specialists in computer systems. The number of possible connections in a period less than a microsecond is in the order of 10,000 to 1,000,000 for a computer. During a period one million times greater, that is, one second, the number increases in relatively modest proportions, approximately 100 times. Moreover, these theoretical possibilities are limited by the number of lines of access to the central memory and the number of units treating information. In other words, the means of the computer are far inferior to those of the human brain.

which it must establish a connection. Sperry removed one eye of an anesthetized toad and regrafted it upside down. Each nerve cell in the retina regenerated the nerve fiber connecting it with the brain, and the retinal cells (even though the eye was upside down) were able to locate unmistakably the brain cells to which they had been linked before the experiment. What extraordinary specificity in recognition! Nothing could better demonstrate that nerve cells have a kind of individuality, personal characteristics which allow them to connect with certain cells, but not with others.

Many other observations, which I do not have the space or the competence to discuss here, have permitted Sperry's successors to affirm that the original characteristics of each nerve cell are registered within its chemical structure at the molecular level, this structure itself having been genetically coded in the program of the cell.

Lord Adrian and the Fly

I should perhaps also mention the electrical activity of the brain. The usual method of recording this activity does not allow a separate study of each neuron. The electroencephalogram, as this recording is called, translates indistinctly the mixed electrical effects of millions of neurons, so that the tracing is something like the confused noise which millions of men would make if they were all talking at once. Yet this rough record, this noise of a crowd so unsuited to detailed analysis, furnishes some information through a certain harmony called synchronization. And some pieces of this information suggest that intellectual activity and brain activity are linked. When the subject is at rest, electrical waves called alpha, with a rhythm of approximately 10 per second, appear on the tracing; but when the subject is engaged in mental arithmetic these alpha waves are replaced by beta waves of lesser amplitude but more rapid rhythm (increasing to 20–30 per second).

In 1934 the distinguished English physiologist, Lord Edgar Douglas Adrian, published his own electroencephalogram in the journal *Brain.* There one can see the electrical waves in the occipital lobe become more frequent and less intense as he opens his eyes. The same phenomenon, he pointed out, can be observed in the cerebral ganglion of the water fly when it passes from the darkness into light— a crude but strange resemblance between the brain of a Nobel laureate in medicine and the brain of a fly.

Animals Have a Brain: Do They Think?

To speak of "thinking" in animals is not farfetched, since animals do not behave like robots. Two animals of the same species have been observed to react differently under what appear to be identical situations. Their behavior may be unpredictable, and each seems to have a personality. This certainly does not mean that the amazing consciousness of self which is characteristic of thinking man exists in animals. But in animals certain mental processes probably underlie the gestures, attitudes, mimicry, and apparently unpredictable behavior which we observe. By analogy with our own mental processes we might call this "animal thinking," provided that we remember that this is no more than a convention, a convenient way of expressing the set of mental phenomena which are reflected in the observed behavior. Only through observing this behavior can we attempt to explore the animal mind, since most animals are not endowed with a language that man can understand.

In man, language is the very expression of his mind. If I had not read or listened to what men say, I would find it very difficult to know what they think. The miracle of human thought is not so much that we are "conscious" of it (the word "conscious" is subjective, hence elusive—it is difficult for us to look at ourselves in our own inner mirror in a purely abstract way); the miracle of human thought is rather that it can be expressed and therefore become infectious, promoting exchanges with other men, and even being transmitted from generation to generation.

We have just said that this means of communication is lacking in animals. In fact, this is not true. It is now well established that a more or less rough form of language exists in many animal species, as we now shall see.

Lip-fish, Dolphins, and Crickets

I have heard the story of the lip-fish, a brilliantly colored fish living in coral reefs, who is also called the cleaner fish because he gathers part of his food from the skin of other fish, removing dead skin and parasites. It seems that the lip-fish uses a sort of language, requesting authorization to approach the big fish he is about to clean in order not to be attacked by it. This language is a dance, with rather well-defined steps, which provokes a positive or negative response from the big fish.

Exchange of signals used by animals living together begins very low on the scale of life. We have seen in Chapter 3 how the transmission of plasmids from one germ to its neighbors "informs" them and helps them resist an antibiotic. When bees want to communicate the location of pollen and nectar to their fellows, they perform a dance in a semicircle on the steps of their beehive.

The dolphin is also a remarkable example of communication between animals. He can emit at least thirty-two different whistling sounds which appear to be key words of a language enabling him to communicate with other dolphins. Recently, books and even movies have dealt with this remarkable phenomenon: *The Day of the Dolphin,* originally written in French by Robert Merle; Cousteau and Diolé's *Dolphins;* and the very recent *Thinking Dolphins, Talking Whales,* by Frank Robson.

The cricket is another transmitter of sounds. He has one song to call his mate, others for copulation (a courting song followed by a triumphal song), still another to announce a battle with a cricket invading his territory, and so on and on. Examples could be indefinitely multiplied. A reader who is particularly interested in this question could pursue it in books written by Donald Griffin, *Listening in the Dark* and *The Question of Animal Awareness.*

There also exist what may be called chemical languages, where an animal releases substances which transmit a message to animals of the same species, and to them alone. An example is the "aphrodisiac pheromone" of certain female butterflies. An incredibly minute dose of one-tenth of a millionth of a gram summons thousands of male butterflies within a radius of three miles. An ant who has found a source of food leaves a chemical trail to alert his fellows. An odor emitted by a male mouse permits a pregnant female to distinguish the male which impregnated her. Strangely enough, the odor of other males disturbs mouse pregnancy; only the odor of the father is tolerated, and some believe that this may play a part in mouse population control.

Another language, as yet little understood, is that used in a colony of insects where communication is established through contact between antennae. It is as if the entire colony formed a unit, each individual bound to the others by invisible links which insure an organized, efficient behavior of the whole.

This social organization closely resembles that of the society of cells making up an individual. Here again, the group can only survive as a closely knit whole, held together through a continuing exchange of information and instructions from cell to cell.

Now let us consider the primates, since the study of their language capacity has furnished the most illuminating data on the mental life of animals.

Washoe and Sarah

In 1966, Beatrice and Allen Gardner took charge of a female chimpanzee named Washoe and undertook to teach her the sign language used by the deaf and dumb. Four years later Washoe was using 132 signs to communicate with the Gardners. Two other American investigators, Ann and David Premack, taught Sarah, another female chimpanzee, 130 different words represented by colored plastic tokens. Through the patience and imagination of these investigators, the ancient dream of communicating with an animal became a reality.

These studies on chimpanzees, as well as studies on psychological reactions of other animals such as dolphins, lead to the following conclusion. Among superior animals, we see simple forms of mental reflection preceding action, the choice of strategy based on probability, the conception of geometric symbols, the development of rational behavior—in short, the basic outline, though imperfect and simple, of the wonderful mechanisms of human thinking. We might compare the universe of animal thought to that of human thought as a small, primitive village to the population of our entire planet, or a few drops of water to the sea. But these little drops of water provide a fascinating model which led to unexpected discoveries in the field of genetic mechanisms involved in the mental activity of animals.

The Genetics of Animal Intelligence

Let us not reopen in this book the eternal question of nature versus nurture. As any impartial observer can testify, the innate and the acquired are both important, and the only real problem concerns the weight to be given to each one. Let us just try to answer the following question: Do the inborn factors influencing animal thinking depend on heredity? Is intellectual activity genetic-dependent as are the other phenomena of life? More precisely, can we find, in the field of the mind, the equivalent of the genetic polymorphism that we have already seen for the body?

This is a vital question, since we have postulated that maintaining sufficient diversity between individuals of the same species is necessary for survival. The import of this idea would be increased tenfold if the entire being, body and thought (or, to put it differently, the body and the functions of the brain), were subject to this natural law.

Unfortunately, research in this field is comparatively recent, and the actual state of our knowledge today does not permit an unequivocal answer. What follows is a brief summary of what we know so far.

In the first part of this book I spoke of the techniques used for the interbreeding of successive generations of mice, creating artificial "pure" strains in which all the mice come to share a more and more similar hereditary material. The method had been so productive in other sectors that it was tempting to use it in the study of behavior. The results are brilliantly clear.

The Education of Mice and Rats

In 1969, Daniel Bovet, working in Rome with his wife and Alberto Oliverio, published the results of a comparison among nine of these "pure" strains of mice. He devised the following test of mental capacity. A mouse is placed in a cage with two compartments, each with a small electric bulb. The bulb lights as a signal; five seconds later the compartment is slightly electrified, and the mouse, finding the electric shock disagreeable, runs into the neighboring compartment. How long will it take the mouse to understand the meaning of the light signal and to leave the cage before the electric shock? DBA/2 mice are so gifted that, as early as the second session of one hundred trials, they avoid the shock four out of ten times. In the following session they succeed eight out of ten times. In comparison, CBA mice learn much more slowly—even after four sessions of one hundred trials they do not achieve more than 10 percent success. Some specialists claim that such experiments do not correctly measure mouse intelligence—differences in emotional reactions might also be involved. But for our purpose this does not matter, since emotions are also an essential component of behavior.

Jacques Larmat cites many similar examples in his excellent little book on the genetics of intelligence. He tells the story of rats finding their way out of a labyrinth. The smartest animals are bred to each other and the most incompetent to each other. This is repeated for several generations, and with the great-great-great-grandchildren the difference between the clever and the incapable families becomes unmistakable. The bright rats, on the average, make less than one error per trial in their search for the exit (getting into one of the dead ends of the labyrinth is counted as an error), while members of the other family make an average of more than five errors per trial.

Other forms of behavior than intelligence also depend on heredity. For instance, Wall, who studied the courting behavior of drakes in the mating season, concluded that the ceremony designed to conquer the female appears to be regulated by the laws of genetics.

The Uniqueness of the Brain
of Each Individual

If heredity plays a part in the functions of the brain, it is fair enough to inquire whether genetic polymorphism can be demonstrated in the brains of individual animals within the same species. This question is clearly raised in the conclusion of Dr. Jerne's speech delivered at the meeting mentioned earlier. Does the same chemical diversity in details exist in the brain as in the heart, the kidney, or the liver? As of today, the answer is definitely affirmative. In fact, however, this diversity among individuals has been demonstrated only for the chemical structures of the brain. It has not yet been proven that these chemical differences are reflected in what we have chosen to call "animal thinking."

As an example, a number of cerebral enzymes have been found to vary slightly from one animal to the next in the same species (for instance, phosphoglucomutase, glucose 6 phosphate dehydrogenase, the enzyme of malic acid, certain esterases, and many others), in contrast to some others which do not vary within a species. (For instance, the enzymes called glycolytic, which attack sugars, did not show any detectable polymorphism in 41 macaque monkeys or in 39 pure strains of mice.) Let me repeat that the role of these enzymes in behavior has not been proved. We can only reason by inference. A good example is the case of the monoamine oxidases commonly known by the abbreviation MAO, which act on "mediators" of nervous transmission.

The MAO probably influence sleep, appetite, and cerebral regulation of body temperature; in man they affect mood—optimism, pessimism—and behavior in mental patients, particularly schizophrenics.* The polymorphism of the MAO in a given species has now been amply verified and its dependence on hereditary factors demonstrated. But that mind and behavior are influenced by an enzyme with a variable structure does not prove that thought will vary with variations in the enzyme.

In short, it is possible (but has not yet been plainly demonstrated) that behavior in individual animals depends, in part, upon brain structures programmed by genetic coding.†

Probably few readers were shocked or even surprised by our recounting these observations made on animals. But I fear they will be less tolerant when we leave the realm of thinking in animals and enter the immense emotional universe where we are both the observers and the observed, the universe of human thought.

---

*I do not want to enter into the highly technical details which underlie these affirmations. I refer the reader who may wish to explore this difficult world of neuroenzymology to works such as those published by Danish researchers, in *Hereditas* (69 [1971], 233, and 70 [1972], 235), on the brain of the teleostomous fish; the article by P. T. Warde Cohen and co-workers in Seattle, which appeared in *Nature New Biology* (241 [1973], 229); or the volume entitled *Neuropsychopharmacology of Monoamines and Their Regulatory Enzymes* (New York: Raven Press, 1974).

†In addition to the chemical polymorphism of brain constituents, one can also conceive fine hereditary variations of cerebral structures. But this field is practically unexplored.

CHAPTER Five

Someone within Me

Quelqu'un qui soit en moi plus moi-même que moi.

—PAUL CLAUDEL, AFTER ST. AUGUSTINE

Human thinking is not simply an amplification of animal thinking: this is what many believe, and I am among them. We have the means to prove that a new, different, and extraordinary happening occurs in man, which we cannot prove to happen in animals. Not only do we think, but we know we are thinking. We have within us both a mind and its witness. Some people call this phenomenon consciousness. An ambiguous word, like any abstract concept, but still the "root of human thought."*

A French philosopher of the last century, Edmond Goblot, wrote: "To be aware is to feel that one feels." And

*Sir William Hamilton, *Lectures on Metaphysics & Logic,* Vol. I.

Jean-Paul Sartre: "The only way for consciousness to exist is being aware of consciousness." You know how philosophers like playing with words and think that in doing so they have found something.

Nevertheless, thinking and knowing that we do so is an exclusive feature of the human species.

Thinking and Language

What about other men? How do we know that they also are in the grip of the strange phenomenon of thought and consciousness? Surely it is because they say so. It is the words, the writings, the mimicry, the language of others which allow us to discover their inner world. All this is quite banal. But I believe we must keep in mind this basic idea: a mute individual can certainly be aware of everything, including the fact that he is mute; but if all men had always been mute—or, rather, had they been mentally mute —they would have been unable to acquire that particular "malady," to use the expression of the Spanish poet Unamuno, which sets us apart from the donkey and the crab, and which we call consciousness. Can one imagine thought without the thought being expressed? It is true that investigators like Jean Piaget have demonstrated that in the human child the dawning of intelligence precedes language. The observations of Sperry, Gazzaniga, and Lhermitte on right-handed individuals suggest also that it is not only the left brain, the seat of language, which takes part in intellectual performances or emotional reactions, but also the right brain, proving that there is thought without language. But if man had never been able to express his thoughts, human thoughts would certainly be different from what they are—deprived of the strange collective impulse coming from the thinking of others, and so infinitely less infectious, less subtle, less penetrating. In short, his thinking would probably be closer to animal thinking as discussed in the preceding chapter.

I apologize to the reader for this digression on a subject which philosophers and neurobiologists have analyzed in more subtle and profound terms. But it appears to me an indispensable premise for what follows: for the scientist who is wary of intangible concepts which have no concrete manifestations and thus escape objective approach, human thought is first and foremost that which can be approached through language.

It so happens that human language provides the most refined tool for gathering information on the deep and dark sources of human behavior. Using it as a tool, we can attempt to answer the following question: What do we know about the possible role of heredity in the thinking and the behavior of man? Is there anything in man similar to the genetic influences on animal minds?

While specialists may crossbreed mice, rats, or ducks as they see fit in order to analyze the role of heredity in animal thought, man does not lend himself to such maneuvers. Here we have only indirect evidence, rarely above criticism. However, a few facts cannot help but strike the imagination.

The Brain in Twins and Adopted Children

Chemically, as we have already pointed out, identical twins derived from one egg start life as two identical individuals, having received the same legacy of hereditary material. Shields studied 88 pairs of identical twins; 44 pairs were raised together, and the other 44 pairs were separated during the first months of life. Intelligence tests showed virtually identical results for identical twins, whether they were raised together or not. Conversely, pairs of fraternal twins showed quite different results, even when they were raised together.

Studies have also compared the intellectual capacity of adopted children to that of their real parents and to that of their adoptive parents.* The answer was again quite clear —a poor IQ correlation between the children and their adoptive parents, a very strong correlation between them and their natural parents. And this is true even if the children had not seen their parents since they were one month old.

In fact, none of these studies is beyond criticism. Everyone is aware of the controversies over the value of so-called intelligence tests. No matter how well designed the test, the measurement of intelligence as a whole is but artificial. Many factors may influence the test, such as size of vocabulary, capacity for putting words together, ability to visualize space, accuracy and rapidity of reasoning, memory, and the

*I am referring to works by Burks, by Leahy, by Erlenmeyer-Kimling and Jarvik, by Skodak and Skeels, by Honzik, and by others.

many other marvelous faculties united under the arbitrary label "intelligence." Ideally, they should all be studied separately.

Hence the problem demands much additional research. We are just at the beginning. Nevertheless, at this point the conclusion reached by the French biologist Jean Rostand in 1925 appears likely to be true: "There is no doubt that human beings are born with genetic differences in the breadth and orientation of their intellectual potential."

If this statement is confirmed in man in the same way it was proven in animals, there can be little reason to doubt that this heredity follows the general laws of diversity discussed in previous chapters under the name of genetic polymorphism. This would not mean that the diversity of behavior and ideas among human beings depends only on genetic influences. On the contrary, this diversity certainly reflects as well the innumerable influences to which each individual has been subjected since birth. But even if inborn potential tendencies play a limited role, it is fascinating to consider as a serious possibility the idea that our brain is partly governed by the amazing genetic laws—in part revealed by research on grafts—which make each individual unique.

The Brain, Yes, but Thinking?

Still, the shortcoming of such conclusions is that they make an ambiguous mixture of the brain and the mind. The reader will say that he is far from being convinced of a correlation between thought processes and molecular structures, and he will be right. He will add that man is neither a toad, nor a mouse, nor even a chimpanzee, and he will be right again. And in the midst of these reflections, the reader is bound to be swayed by his own view of the world.

He may, for instance, have decided once and for all to deny that his soul and his inner life have the slightest relationship to the function of his brain cells. He will consider it a sacrilege that beauty, love, generosity, or the idea of justice should ever be expressed in terms of molecular chemistry. Rightly, he will recall the somewhat naïve theory of "scientism" developed at the end of the last century. The followers of scientism were so enthusiastic about the progress of science that they were prepared to swear that nothing in the world would remain impervious to it. And the major error was to believe that science would explain not only the how but also the why. This reader might underline how dangerous it would be to make thinking dependent on physicochemical phenomena, because if the brain secreted thought in the same way that the liver secretes bile, our heads and our actions would be bound by an implacable determinism, a kind of inevitable destiny. And all the nobility of the human soul, the possibilities of creation, the mysteries of innermost emotions, the feeling of what is right and wrong, the concept of free will and responsibilities, liberty and limitless spiritual adventures—in one word, all the wonder of human life—would be lost.

Other readers, however, will not understand why it is forbidden to relate the science of the brain to the mysteries of the soul; they will not see the sacrilege in such an approach. They will say that the misunderstanding comes precisely from those naïve enthusiastic times when, drunk with the gigantic advances of science, one did not perceive the limits by which science is bound. They will insist that sci-

ence, far from being a machine to give the world significance, is only a method to explore the world. They will
even point out that the scientific method contrasts with
other facets of the human mind, such as faith, or art, because
its rules are totally different: it tries to be a mirror of the
outside world, with as little subjective distortion as possible,
and it insists that facts are "true" only in respect to the
conditions under which they have been observed. Science
cannot be the source of absolute truth, but only a technique
for research into relative truths. Therefore, this second
group of readers will see no obstacle to the scientific study
of the relation between the brain and the mind. And they
will refuse to predict what can come out of this study, for
the accomplishments of science are both limited and unpredictable. Because one cannot predict the results of the study
of the brain, the possibility remains that someday sufficient
progress will be made for the structures and movement of
thought to be correlated with the structures and chemical
functions of the brain.

Obviously a deep gulf divides these two paths of reflection, the same breach which separates psychology and
neurobiology. Each party ignores the other, and when they
are confronted with each other the discussion becomes
heated.

And still I believe, as so often is the case, that this controversy rests on a misunderstanding, on an inaccurate analysis
of what we know today.

A Freedom Born of Numbers

Even if the brain is the instrument of thought, it is false to believe that this would imply a total determinism, a total lack of freedom. Just stop and think about the profound change that the progress of scientific thought has brought about in the concept of determinism. The physicists first, then all the other scientific disciplines, have seen clearly that once a phenomenon depends on factors sufficiently numerous and intricate (including those which involve the relationship of the observer to the object observed), the scientific method no longer dictates a conclusion in terms of certainties, but rather (at best) in terms of probabilities.

The result is that even with relatively crude computers fed a limited amount of data, effects of apparent spontaneity can appear, unexpected even by the programmer. The machine escapes him, so to speak. In the brain, the number of units is infinitely greater. Each neuron is made up of innumerable original molecules of unknown and possibly limitless potential. There are more than 10 billion neurons in the brain. Let us imagine that the secret links joining the molecular functioning of neurons and certain steps in thinking will be discovered someday. The incredible number of neuron elements involved would make it quite impossible that thought could be forecast from mere physicochemical data. Therefore, such data will not preclude the necessity for research of a totally different nature: psychological, sociological, and ethical approaches to human thought.

Thus the rivalry between neurobiology and psychology

is fruitless and counterproductive. We are dealing with two distinct methods. They are not incompatible, they are just different. Confusion could stem from forgetting the clear-cut distinction between these two methods, not from seeking links between the brain and the mind.

The Dream of the Poet and the Dream of the Biologist

To show how meaningless this rivalry is, and to prove that each approach has a validity independent of the other, let me use the example of dreams.

On pages 98 and 99 texts of poets and psychologists on the left confront texts of neurobiologists on the right.

The first of these pages inspires my admiration for the nimbleness of the human brain, the profundity and beauty of poetic inspiration, and the intelligence of psychologists. The second page, which is closer to my field, has no relevance to the search for beauty. The scientist, far from seeking emotion, rather fears its intrusion. He is guided only by the rules of observation and humility before the facts, the very rules of the scientific method. The page on the left is no less true than the one on the right if we take the word "truth" to mean that which ranks high in our personal scale of values. ("That is true which suits man," wrote Thomas Mann in *The Magic Mountain*. "We know the truth not only through reason but also through the heart," Pascal had said earlier. And Keats wrote, "What the imagination seizes as beauty must be truth.") But the second page, contrary to the first, only stands modestly looking for another kind of truth, much more limited, more independent from our emotional personality. We are dealing with two points of view, two sets of rules for two different games, two different languages. There is no more contradiction between them than there is between music and the manufacture of stringed instruments. Bach and Mozart are no less great, no less necessary because in the musical scale the A note corresponds to 440 vibrations per second. But there is a difference: some men may be insensitive to the beauties of *The Well-Tempered Clavier* or *The Magic Flute,* but none can question that 440 vibrations per second characterize the sound which musicians call A.

The Birth of Freedom

From sound to music, from a well-tempered scale to *The Well-Tempered Clavier,* from a block of marble to the *Venus of Milo,* from the letters of the alphabet to Hamlet's soliloquy there is no doubt an ascent. The astonishing progression in which atoms make molecules, molecules make cells, cells make organs, organs make bodies has as a final achievement in the human species the explosion of an intriguing spiritual world. François Jacob compared the degrees of this progression to Russian dolls fitting within each other, ever larger and larger. *Integrons* is the word he uses for these degrees in the story of life.

What is different about human thought is an additional capacity for abstraction or, if one prefers, liberty. It does not matter whether we describe the human mind in terms of phenomena or in terms of mysteries. The end result in

"Absurd, incongruous dreams, those dreams that I call hieroglyphics, of course belong to the supernatural part of life."

—Charles Baudelaire

"[Dreams] have a weight upon our waking thoughts,
They take a weight from our waking toils
They do divide our being; they become
A portion of ourselves as of our time,
And look like heralds of eternity."

—Lord Byron

"Oft morning dreams presage approaching fate,
For morning dreams, as poets tell, are true."

—Michael Bruce

"Dreams, you know, go always by contraries."

—Oliver Goldsmith

"The dream is the aquarium of the night."

—Victor Hugo

"To dream is to sleep with illustrations in the text."

—Eugène d'Ors y Rovira

"[The dream] is the best performance I know."

—Eugène Ionesco

"A dream that is not understood, says the Talmud, is like an unopened letter."

—Blake Clark

"Dreaming permits each and every one of us to be quietly and safely insane every night of our lives."

—William Dement

"[Dreams], the Royal Way to the subconscious."

—Sigmund Freud

"Dreams can sometimes announce events long before they happen. What escapes from our conscious world is often caught by our subconscious, which can inform us through our dreams."

—Carl Gustav Jung

During the course of eight hours of sleep, man first becomes much less sensitive to touch, then the depth of sleep begins to lighten through five successive waves. At the summit of each wave is a period when the electroencephalogram shows a special tracing resembling that of waking. These short periods are associated with rapid eye movements (the term "rapid-eye-movement [REM] sleep" is often used) and with a complete relaxation of the other muscles of the body (paradoxically contrasting with the electric tracing of waking, hence another name, "paradoxical sleep"). Now, if the sleeper is awakened during any of these periods of REM or paradoxical sleep, 80 times out of 100 he will remember that he was in the middle of a dream; if he is awakened at any other time, 93 times out of 100 he will assure you that he was not dreaming.

The details of these figures, found by Kleitman together with Dement and Aserinski, are questioned by some, but everyone agrees that dreaming occurs almost exclusively during these periods and is a normal, rhythmic phenomenon, like heartbeats, respiration, and sleep itself. Jouvet and his co-workers, who were pioneers in this research and who coined the term "paradoxical sleep," have shown that this phenomenon depends upon the associated action of "the posterior raphe complex" and the "locus coeruleus" of the brain, triggered by chemical mechanisms involving serotonin and noradrenalin. They also discovered that the phenomenon, like so many other biological phenomena, is genetically determined and has a standard evolution during the course of a lifetime.

In the *British Medical Journal* of January 13 and February 10, 1973, it is reported that the drug Nitrazepam, used as a sleeping pill, can provoke vivid and painful nightmares. The comment reads: Throughout history some men in very important positions have allowed their dreams to influence their actions, and the same is no doubt the case in modern times. If a world leader who was influenced by such fantasies were to dream, as a result of taking Nitrazepam . . . that he was divinely inspired to take a certain course of action, the consequences obviously could be serious. The doctor who prescribed the tablets might unwittingly have changed world history, and not necessarily for the better.

either case will be the same. Those who prefer to think in terms of mystery will say, I believe, that this kind of liberty is too wonderful to be studied by the biological methods used for the human body. They will insist that thought is and will remain totally mysterious and defy analysis in terms of physical chemistry. If they are believers, human thought will be central to their faith. "We are dominated by the persistent illusion," wrote Teilhard de Chardin, "that the flame rises out of the depths of the earth and is lighted progressively along the brilliant wake of life. Lord, you have given me grace to understand that this vision is false and that in order to perceive You I must reverse it. In the beginning was Power, intelligent, loving, and active. In the beginning was the Word, entirely capable of dominating and molding whatever came into being. In the beginning cold and darkness did not exist, there was the Flame. This is the truth."

Those, on the other hand, who conceive the mind in terms of phenomena, will say that our feeling of liberty, including the liberty of saying No, only reflects the multitude of influences, connections, pathways, and crossroads of our thinking; liberty is but the reflection of the immeasurable complexity of our cerebral activity. To quote François Jacob once more: "In man the number of possible responses becomes so great that one may speak of that 'free will' so dear to philosophers." The freedom of creation, the freedom of decision would be the natural consequence of an infinite number of influences, inborn or environmental, which direct the way. The number of these factors is so great as to defy analysis and to make the direction taken appear to be the result of spontaneous choice.

What, indeed, is this famous freedom if not the fact that we do not know ahead of time what decisions we are to make? We have no idea, before experiencing them, whether life in the country or the works of Picasso will give us pleasure. Once more, I repeat, we can approach the mind only through its manifestations. The freedom of choice in our thinking can be discussed only in terms of the manifestations of this freedom. When I look at one of Picasso's portraits of women, I am beset with many contradictory feelings evidently coming from the complexity hidden behind the apparent simplicity of the drawing. For a moment, perhaps for several minutes, I do not know myself whether the feelings of admiration or the feelings of dislike will prevail within me. Thus the phenomenon of unpredictability can be created by a sufficient amount of information and a sufficient complexity of its processing.

Let me illustrate this in another way. Consider the instruments invented by man and apparently endowed with more and more spontaneous behavior. Man started by building automatic machines where everything was ordered ahead of time and nothing left to chance: for example, calculating machines where two and two always make four. During the last few centuries he has devised the most varied and marvelous automated devices, such as the mechanical lion programmed by Leonardo da Vinci to greet Louis XII as he entered Milan. Then came the invention of control systems, where the goal of the machine is fixed but the timing and schedule are not. For example, Edmund Lee in England invented in 1745 a small pilot windmill, equipped with a fantail, to keep a large windmill facing into the wind. Whenever the direction of the wind changed, the fantail would turn the large windmill into the wind, so that maximum power was always provided. Another example would be the centrifugal governor invented by James Watt in 1787 in order to maintain the speed of a steam engine at a chosen level. In the same way today, the thermostat operates spontaneously whenever triggered by information it receives on room temperature. A further step in the liberation of the machine is the computer, endowed with memory, programs, methods of calculating, logical mechanisms, possibilities of modifying its course according to information received at any moment, "language" devices to express results or to command other machines. This certainly does not mean that the computer is endowed with true "freedom," since two computers programmed in the same fashion and receiving identical input will act identically. The computer is slave to the program it receives. But it is clear that in human beings the mental "program" differs from one man to the next, varying with both inborn and acquired diversity. And it is also clear that if two computers, even identical (which, as we know, is not the case for two human brains), were programmed in an only slightly different fashion, the response of each computer would be different. One would have the illusion that computers act with free will.

"I will grant," you may object, "that man has been clever enough to create these marvelous instruments. But to equate the apparent freedom of these machines with the true freedom of human creativity is to mistake a talking doll for a living baby. The computer has logic, but there is a great deal more than logic in the living baby."

True freedom, or apparent freedom? The debate echoes across the centuries. To St. Bernard de Clairvaux, who wrote in the twelfth century that "free will not only elevates man above all living creatures, but also allows him to reign over them," Jacques Monod, eight hundred years later, answers that all the innermost workings of our minds depend simply on "changes in the shape of billions and billions of little molecular crystals."

The controversy in some respects resembles a quarrel among players, some of whom want to play cricket, while the others want to play baseball. In this case we are playing with two different sets of rules for the use of the word "freedom," but I would suggest that there is no necessary contradiction between the belief in true free will and the search for a biological basis for this feeling of freedom: the Russian dolls may require different approaches and *still* fit within each other.

Let us now leave this eternal debate behind us. Both sides must admit that human thought, the latest arrival among the Russian dolls, the most interesting and the most formidable, takes off on its own and is able to generate independent action. This birth of liberty, whatever meaning is attributed to the word, indicates that we are no longer passive. Seeing what we see around us, the strange games and rules of nature, we are reminded of Paul Tillich writing, "Man can ask questions and give answers." And the answer can be No. The greater the freedom of thought, the greater the possibilities of going against the established order; creation signifies the capacity for revolt. And if man uses his brain to say No, he can at the same time use his brain to transform the No into acts. Man has acquired the means of producing immeasurable changes in the world in which he lives, changes which may run contrary to natural laws. Prometheus gave man fire—the fire that both lights the void and may destroy the world.

CHAPTER  *Six*

Playing with Fire

Here, then, is man. A strange living being. On the one hand, as in all other species, each human individual has his own original and unique personality. Not only in his body, but perhaps even in his brain, his behavior, his thought. On the other hand, man differs from all other species by the advent of a spiritual universe which adds an explosive new dimension, expanding both toward logic and toward emotion.

Logic has created the scientific method, a method for the quest of truth. Not absolute truth. But rather a limited truth, voluntarily restricted by the very rules of the game, requiring verification and hence capable of gaining universal acceptance.

Emotion, on the other hand, is the source of a different host of human thoughts, a world of unlimited horizon in our quest to give our life significance, in our search for beauty, faith, love, and happiness. A wonderful world, but subjective, personal, differing from one man to another, a world that, contrary to science, does not tend toward unanimity. A world that is the true motor of a free human action, unpredictable, unregulated, escaping the slavery of animal behavior.

This double explosion of the human mind, toward science and toward the world of emotions, has endowed man with a unique power. He is the only living species that can alter the world in which he lives, and even his own fate.

This is not the place to discuss the many emotional forces which engender human action. Analyzing this subjective world, we would have to go from love to hate, from joy to grief, from spiritual visions to the search for happiness. This is the same world where flourish so many wonders, from poetry to music. Like most men, I marvel at all these wonders, but I am not competent to discuss them. Therefore I will limit myself to the field of biology, which happens to be a good example of how human freedom, including the freedom to say No, may trouble the natural mechanisms of the evolution of life.

An Appetite for Justice

I hope that by now the reader is convinced that in all living species, including man, the uniqueness of each individual is not just a whim of nature. It plays an essential role in the survival of the species. The plurality of individuals, their disparity, their inequality, are almost certainly factors of species survival in the game of natural selection. The way this game works is shocking to us because it is based on the elimination of the weak (meaning individuals who adapt badly to a given environment) and on the survival of the strong (the fittest, who best resist hostile conditions). This natural role of inequality is bound to offend the deepest aspirations of the human spirit: our appetite for justice, our inclination to defend the lone individual, and our wish that all men be equal as they face life.

Is it necessary to recall that such feelings are found only in the human species, not in any other living being? Ethics and the notion of good and evil do not exist except in the human. That it is wrong to kill one's neighbor does not occur to a bee when it follows the rule of its species that any superfluous queen be put to death immediately. The idea of good and evil means nothing to the hatchery-raised apistogram fish that Konrad Lorenz observed devouring his eggs and progeny. We could cite a hundred other examples. Human morality, which condemns injustice, inequality, cruelty, simply does not apply to the animal world. In the case of animals the aim appears quite different: survival, individual survival, and above all survival of the species. Indeed, the animal is perhaps even programmed in the light of a broader scheme, the maintenance of a general equilibrium among all living species. I am alluding to stories like that of the moose and wolves on Isle Royale in Lake Superior.

During a very severe winter when the lake froze over, a bridge of ice formed between the island and the Canadian mainland, allowing the moose to cross over. On the island they found a paradise—rich pasture and not a single wolf. They multiplied to such an extent that the formerly abundant vegetation became scarce and the moose population began to suffer from famine. In order to deal with this overpopulation, the forest rangers introduced a few wolves provided by a neighboring zoo—well-behaved wolves who refused to chase the moose and were finally returned to their zoo. The following winter was again exceptionally cold. The lake froze once more, and this time a band of wild wolves crossed the ice to the island. They started to hunt down the moose, killing the weakest and the undernourished. Today the island population has reached a natural equilibrium, with approximately three hundred moose and twenty-five wolves—three hundred moose who do not run the risk of famine because the wolves control their number, killing and devouring the surplus.

Thus, with the advances of biology, the rules developed through the generous and passionate aspirations of man under the name of ethics reveal more and more clearly their true significance, which is a revolt against the natural order, a refusal to obey passively the normal laws of evolution and survival.

The Human Adventure

Both the spice and the nobility of the human adventure stem from this refusal. What would our miserable existence amount to if men turned away from this gift of liberty brought by the human mind? The fact is, they do not. While no animal apparently rebels against his destiny, we, on the contrary, never cease to express through behavior and language our rebellion against the contradiction between the world as it is and the world we dream of.

It is possible that this rebellion may sometimes account for man's worst individual excesses, as the psychologist Erich Fromm suggests when he qualifies aggression and cruelty as one of the ways man tries to "make sense out of life." But for the majority of men the refusal to follow natural law comes under the heading of ethics. It is grossly unfair that some men and women should be struck by sickness and suffering while others live to a ripe old age in good health. So medicine is born. It is grossly unfair that man may injure, even kill his neighbor with impunity, so the rules for rights and justice among men are born. It is grossly unfair that there should be the weak and the strong, the master and the slave, and this is the seed of social progress. In the writings of all the moralists I have read, and in my own thinking, it is clear that these impulses arise spontaneously from the depths of our being. They come from within ourselves rather than being imposed from outside. Indeed, perhaps the majority of men believe that without these bursts of spiritual endeavor life itself would not be worth living (although the scene around us may throw some doubt on this). "Man has no alternative but to set as his goal the regression of the suffering in the world," wrote Camus in *The Revolt of Man.* "But even if limited, injustice and suffering will always exist, and it will never cease to be a scandal. The 'why' of Dimitri Karamazov will continue to reverberate. As long as a single man remains . . . rebellion will not die."

People may read the above lines on the human spirit inspiring human action and say: "Here is another Candide, arguing that we live in the best of all possible worlds. Why not rather be impressed by the increasing poverty of our spiritual life. Moral conscience is growing weaker. Men kill, steal, scoff at morality centuries old. Little by little we are losing the satisfaction which comes from the ability to wonder, and the sight of an honest and friendly face no longer inspires us with a warm and exalted feeling."

All this is true of some people, but I insist it is not true for everyone. Of course, even if it were true for only one man in a thousand, it would still be disturbing, because one man alone can cause great harm. But it happens that we speak more about thieves, murderers, and dictators than about non-thieves, non-murderers, and non-dictators. Besides, concerning this thousandth man, it might be well to return to one of the ideas developed in the first chapters of this book, the thousandth mosquito.

The Thousandth Mosquito Revisited

Out of one thousand mosquitoes there will be one who is different enough from the others to refuse to succumb to DDT. Let me point out in parentheses that the species is saved by this thousandth mosquito. But this is not our concern here. We are focusing on an individual mosquito who reacts differently from the mass of his companions; and this may help to clarify the problem of the man who, in a given domain, is not entirely the same as other men.

The simplest example of the man who is outside the norm

is found among those suffering from a hereditary disease. Everyone is familiar with the harelip, a deformity which splits the upper lip in two like that of a hare. We know today that this malformation is almost always the result of a "genetic mutation." There are other "hereditary" exceptions, like some dwarfs, some patients with eye and brain diseases, multiple kidney cysts, anemias, and a number of innate errors of metabolism—functional defects affecting one of the innumerable chemical reactions which are the warp and woof of human bodily function. Here is an example.

An infant is born, blond and blue-eyed, apparently normal. Several weeks later, he develops eczema and has digestive troubles and convulsions. Soon it becomes evident that the child is abnormally restless and that his intelligence is not developing. The doctor discovers that the child's urine contains phenylpyruvic acid and other derivatives of phenylalanine. (The disease is called phenylketonuria.)

We know now that the disease results from a lack of transformation of phenylalanine into tyrosine, a normal route in the degradation of body proteins. Phenylalanine then accumulates in amounts ten, twenty, thirty times greater than in the healthy child, and this produces irreversible brain damage. If this accumulation is diagnosed and treated soon enough by a special diet, the child will be protected from mental retardation.

It should be pointed out that this disease remained rare (less than 1 in 10,000 infants) because most of these children died young without transmitting the defect. But now when a child is miraculously saved by treatment, he will grow up to marry, to procreate, and so to pass the hereditary abnormality to future generations. I will return later to this typical example of how a moral imperative, saving these children, opposes a natural law, protecting the species against the spread of a hereditary disease.

Medicine today provides many other examples of individuals who are not altogether the same as others. If the reader has followed our description of the sophisticated system controlling the tree of human heredity and the key role of mutations, he will no doubt find it natural that some individuals *must* be outside the norm.

Can one extrapolate these observations to the human brain, and perhaps even to human behavior? We have already stressed that great caution is still necessary in this field. What follows must therefore be considered hypothetical. But we cannot avoid giving some thought to the subject, because it is fundamental to the understanding of most of the present problems of the human community.

When we observe the behavior of some men, clearly different from that of others, the image of the thousandth mosquito again comes to mind. Might it not apply to exceptional people, whether genius or criminal? Wouldn't a Beethoven, a Pasteur, or an Einstein be a thousandth mosquito? Are the great political leaders quite the same as other men? At the other end of the spectrum, might not megalomania, hypomania, paranoia, delinquency, and criminality also reflect extremes of human potential, which may surface or remain submerged, depending on circumstances?

It will be said, quite correctly, that so far this mental polymorphism is by no means proved to be genetic-dependent. Still, we do know now that certain mental abnormalities such as manic-depressive psychosis are dependent upon heredity. Similar conclusions have been reached by Professor Seymour Kety at Harvard Medical School, and by others, concerning another severe mental disorder, schizophrenia. Twin concordance and other studies support the idea that schizophrenic patients have at least a genetic predisposition.

According to investigators like F. J. Kallman, homosexuality is a behavior enhanced by genetic factors. In a study of 37 pairs of identical twins, he found that when one twin was homosexual, the other always shared the tendency, whereas in 26 sets of fraternal twins (therefore biologically distinct), the twin of the homosexual usually showed no interest in homosexuality. It is important to emphasize that in all such cases environmental factors are at least as important as genetic predisposition. The respective weight of the inherited versus the acquired is today a subject of intense debate, sometimes more political than scientific. But for our purposes here, it is enough to say that both must be taken into account.

For instance, movies and television day after day show scenes of violence, casual murders, daring robberies, the taking of hostages. It is tempting to conclude that such images of violence are a direct cause of the increase in the violence of our everyday lives. Who can escape such a pervasive influence? Well, I am not quite sure that this is the whole picture. It is reasonable to think that 999 people out of 1,000 will *not* be driven to violence by watching violence on the screen. They will react in a healthy manner and keep their balance. But just as the insecticide reveals the thousandth mosquito who does not react like the others, the thousandth man may turn out to be more easily influenced by what he sees on the screen and feel compelled to act it out, often in the greatest detail. Were this hypothesis correct, it would not resolve the problem. Should one forbid the show to the 999 individuals who are able to tolerate it perfectly, under the pretext that the thousandth will be contaminated? What signs would point him out in advance? And, in any case, how could one prevent his seeing TV or the movies? At first glance I see no solution. But problems should be stated clearly even if no immediate key can be found. Nothing is more urgent today than a clear and healthy grasp of the problems facing us.

With Open Eyes

A clear and healthy grasp of problems. Is this possible, in a world and at a time overridden by a bewildering array of problems?

The biologist is tempted to say that the central problem of mankind has taken the form of a conflict. The protagonists in this conflict must be explicitly defined. One is natural biological law. The other is man's spiritual aspirations, including a host of wishes running counter to natural law.

The purpose of this book was to give examples of the rules of this natural law, examples originating in recent research in transplantation. Natural law decrees that children born with a hereditary defect must die, that the life of individuals with hereditary polycystic kidneys should be brief and end in a long and painful agony. This we feel is unfair. We ask medicine to right this wrong. And it does so. Medicine today can replace destroyed kidneys, and those who before were condemned to death can live as long a life as other men. This is an example of a successful battle in our struggle against nature, its injustice and cruelty.

But in making these conquests man is playing with fire. Since the turn of the century, prevention and cure of disease have brought the average duration of life from 50 years to 75 years and infant mortality from 10 in 100 to 2 in 100. Excellent. This, however, has upset the demographic equilibrium. It took a million years for the human population to reach 3 billion; it will take only thirty-five years to double this figure. Not only has the number of men populating the earth tremendously increased, but the age pyramid has been deeply modified as its summit, represented by the aged, grows from year to year.

In the same manner, preventing the natural death of children with hereditary defects increases the incidence of the defect when the patient matures, marries, and procreates. We have given the example of phenylketonuria. If we consider all the diseases influenced by heredity—diabetes, hypertension, mental disease, and many others—it becomes clear that the new advances in medicine carry the risk of a rapid extension of these diseases from generation to generation.

Hence medicine is a good example of the conflict opposing nature to the human rebellion against natural injustice. Nature's schemes and mankind's dreams have different purposes. And yet pacific coexistence is necessary. It is necessary because nature might otherwise exact such severe penalties that all our successes would come to naught. I speak of medicine because it is my profession, but the ecologist, the chemist, the historian, perhaps even the politician, could certainly furnish similar examples.

———

Paying the Piper

From the wars among men we learn that there is never a winner, there are only losers. Let us beware lest in the conflict between man and nature both should be losers. If we decide to combat a natural law which is contrary to our spiritual aspirations, we have to make provision that nature is not unduly affected by our victory. A difficult problem but not insoluble once it is clearly stated. This will of course be a long-term project. In each step of the battle we will have to pay the price. There is no struggle without sacrifice.

In practice these sacrifices will come at different prices.

In many circumstances the moral tendencies of man are not very far distant from the imperatives of natural evolution. In some cases they are virtually identical. Take, as a first example, incest. Here the most remote traditions, the commands of all religions, and some sort of innermost, unexplained force all converge toward the same ethical rule: "No man shall approach a blood relation for intercourse." This happens to be exactly what a biologist in charge of the future of the human species would have decreed. We have seen that if blood relatives were to propagate, this would jeopardize genetic polymorphism, a key to species survival.

Along the same lines, human migrations or individual movements about the globe obviously appeal to most men. This, too, finds favor with the biologist, who knows that it will increase the variety of marriages and the mixture of chromosomes.

A third example: Racism. The biologist has the proof in hand that the concept of pure human races, some superior to others, has not the slightest scientific basis. In fact, he knows that if any small group, considering themselves an elite, were to create what specialists call isolates, this would in the long run be suicidal for them. A good illustration is the story of the descendants of Queen Victoria. She carried a genetic mutation capable of transmitting hemophilia. This mutation was a disaster because her descendants followed the royal custom of intermarrying in order to preserve pure royal blood. And this royal blood killed them: Leopold of Albania, son of Queen Victoria; Frederick of Hesse, son of Alice of England and the Grand Duke of Hesse; Leopold and Maurice, sons of Beatrice of England and Henry of Battenberg; Tsarevitch Alexis of Russia, son of Alexandra of Hesse and Tsar Nicholas II; Waldemar and Henry, sons of Irene of Hesse and Henry of Prussia; Alfonso and Gonzales, sons of Victoria Eugenia and King Alfonso XIII of Spain. All these, and others, received carefully selected noble blood, protected from any misalliance. All of them were hemophilic, and most of them died before the age of twenty.

Other problems are more difficult. They may be exemplified by the demographic explosion. At first glance our desire that no man die before his time is paid for by an enormous and dangerous overpopulation of the globe. But this is a good example of those cases where we have the means of controlling the side effects of a wonderful achievement. The means is well known now. It runs into obstacles, it is not easily applied everywhere, it meets prejudice, but it does exist. Its name is birth control. Birth control can even be complemented if mankind responds to overpopulation by a better management of natural resources and food production.

This, of course, will not solve another demographic problem, the propagation of hereditary diseases in future generations. But here again prevention is possible even while saving the lives of affected children. The means is the creation of genetic counseling. This idea is growing everywhere in the world, and special centers provide advice to couples who know of hereditary diseases in their families. There are more than two hundred such centers in the United States alone. More than 3 million newborn Americans are tested each year for phenylketonuria, the hereditary anomaly discussed earlier. A large U.S. laboratory uses automatic systems for simultaneous detection of a whole series of hereditary diseases on just one blood or urine sample. In many cases it is now possible to predict the percentage of risk of transmitting a given hereditary disease to the next generation. The couple who apply to a genetic counselor are informed of the exact risk, and without any coercion they usually accept the wisest course—no children if the risk is too high. The Edinburgh Genetic Centre reports that 95 percent of couples decide not to have children if the risk of abnormality is greater than 10 percent. Other centers, we must admit, sometimes publish less encouraging results: couples informed of an enormous risk still do nothing to avoid having children; others, who run only negligible risk, become so frightened that they decide to remain childless, and every effort to persuade them to the contrary is in vain. But apart from these rare cases, no one can doubt the efficacy of genetic counseling.

Other problems, we must confess, are farther from solution. Remember the thousandth human mosquito. Whether he is a minor delinquent or a powerful dictator, a solution is not easy to find because any course must respect the other kind of thousandth mosquito, the species of Mozart, Shakespeare, and the Curies, without whom the human adventure would not be what it is.

In brief, many of the new problems do have possible solutions. Others do not yet. But there is no evidence that any one of these difficulties will be eternally insoluble. On the contrary, if the problems are clearly stated, there is every reason to believe that the astounding human intelligence has the capacity of finding compromises between our spiritual aspirations and the laws of nature. I firmly believe that we can find solutions that will respect at the same time the great expectations of the human soul and the rules protecting the survival of living species, as disclosed by recent advances in biology. Indeed, seeking and finding such solutions might alleviate man's sense of insecurity and frustration and create a new harmony between us and the world.

But it is easier to find solutions on paper than to put them into practice. Even if all the peoples of the world lived under enlightened governments, these would remain impotent if their solutions were not supported by the people. Politicians have come to realize that they need the moral pressure of the majority to be effective. The impulse must come from the public. The solutions must be found with their participation. That is the greatest difficulty, the stiffest price, the most dubious battle.

Reasonable Creatures Insensitive to Reason

One thing is certain (at least to a physician, but probably also to any impartial observer): that men will not be moved by reason alone. Exhort a man or a people with logical reasons, and look at the results: failure, nine times out of ten.

Do you know the story of whale fishing? As the whales of the world, especially the beautiful blue whales, were increasingly threatened by unregulated fishing, the International Whaling Commission was formed in 1949. The Commission designated a Scientific Committee. Prolonged studies, lively discussions, and much hard work eventually led the Scientific Committee to a plan which could save the whale. Alas, the plan remained a dead letter.

The reason was that the International Whaling Commission, like so many international organizations, cannot force a country to do anything it does not want to do.* Still, the Scientific Committee would not admit defeat. Every year in June the International Whaling Commission would meet and the Committee would try to persuade the Commission members to accept the plan. Every year they would fail. The Commission voted and did not achieve the required three-

---

*The regulations of the International Whaling Commission state that "the decisions are not binding except in the countries which have presented no objections within the following ninety days; they do not apply to countries having presented an objection as long as this objection has not been withdrawn." Article VIII of these regulations also states, "Any country has the right to disregard the regulations accepted hitherto, by advising the Commission of the reasons for its decision."

quarters majority. Or when it did, some countries just refused to conform to the decision. And these countries, by a strange coincidence, were those who made the highest profit from the products of whale fishing. In 1965 the Scientific Committee announced that the massacre of blue whales had reached the critical point. The species was about to become extinct. The appeal to reason had not been sufficient to counterbalance the weight of the rubles and yen flowing from the catch.

But this is not the end of the story. After the appeal to reason had failed, the whale began to receive fervent sentimental support. It came from everywhere: societies for the protection of nature, books and pamphlets, international congresses in Stockholm and elsewhere. The media carried the story to the public (and, please note, sometimes in excessive terms). Such a strong movement developed that the International Whaling Commission was forced to give in. Fishing for the few blue whales which had escaped the massacre was finally forbidden, and today patient efforts are rebuilding the threatened species. This seems to me a fine example of the fact that man, endowed with reason, is led by sentiment.

So let us forget reason for a moment and turn to sentiment. Let us acknowledge that crowds—men, women, adolescents—are moved by fervor, not by logic. Even in the West, where science was born of logic, men continue to refuse the arguments of reason and to prefer mystical appeals, whether admirable or illusory. It is as if they sought an escape into irrational worlds. Think of the masses at Woodstock or the Isle of Wight. Think of men and women seeking nirvana in drugs. I am sure that you will find many other examples with one single explanation: the desire to escape from the rational world. People have even been tempted to oppose poetry to science (though they are wonderfully complementary), to claim that poetry is the source of all peace and happiness while science is making our world cheerless.

What I have tried to stress in this book is that there are much nobler adventures to propose to mankind, and the greatest of these is the struggle which seeks to impose human ethics on the inhuman rules of the world. This, I must insist, is not a purely rational adventure. It gives meaning to our lives. Our quest is to imprint an irrational human stamp on the brutal logic of the natural world. And this is no small undertaking. The question is whether enough people can become passionately concerned. I believe that this is the responsibility of Western civilization and that the time has come to place this problem above all others.

Need I say that the biologist and the physician cannot solve this problem? They can only offer a few preliminary thoughts.

A Time for Reflection

There is a first obstacle to such a spiritual awakening: modern man is a fragmented being, distracted by a thousand unimportant things which leave no time for meditation. George Bernard Shaw opened one of his lectures with these words: "I suppose that you seldom think. Very few people think more than three or four times a year. I myself owe my fame to the fact that I think once or twice a week."

Thinking is more and more discouraged by a kind of pollution at the very time when, as we saw, reflection has become essential to any satisfactory evolution of the human community. Silence and solitary meditation have gradually been taken from us by never-ending interference, from the TV at home to the transistor radio outside. It is as if we feared to be alone with ourselves and were trying to escape any occasion to meditate. Even our leisure seems organized toward oblivion rather than reflection. Yet the value of meditation was not discovered yesterday: meditation has been taught by oriental philosophers for thousands of years. I remember once, during a trip to Japan, visiting those gardens where men remain immobile, immersed in their inner world; or those narrow huts where for more than seven centuries the Chanu yu rite and tea ceremony have demanded that the visitor leave all unrest behind. There it occurred to me that if, during the course of his short life, the Parisian, the New Yorker, or the Londoner were to rediscover the art of meditation, he also might be tempted to renew acquaintance with himself and the relations between himself and the world. This is not a matter of the organization of our society, people will say. Governments cannot impose meditation. Perhaps not, but at least they can refrain from putting obstacles in the way. Using the magical means of mass media, some regimes shackle free thought and replace it with collective conditioning. In the so-called liberal societies, the mass media have, fortunately, less the aim of conditioning our minds, but still they invade our lives and consume our days with so much entertainment, distraction, advertising, scandal, serials, poor science fiction, or excellent shows that there is little time left for quiet reflection. What is this if not pollution?

The Struggle

If man finds time to think about his adventure, the feeling may grow that life is worth fighting for.

Let us forget the details and stick to the essential. Biology uncovers a world of cruelty in which we are engaged on every front. Through an extraordinary burst of human thought, which biology only half understands, a rebellion has been born within us which rejects nature's lack of pity, which demands almost impossible crusades for justice, equality between men, suppression of disease, and other transgressions of natural laws. Hurrah for this rebellion! It gives meaning to human existence. But today we realize how great the tact, the subtlety, the prudence required in order not to spoil everything by violating a natural equilibrium which is no less essential for the survival of mankind. This is the human crusade, with all its wonders and its difficulties. Every human being must understand that this is a struggle, and indeed the only true struggle of man. He must take the time. He must find the means. And the whole of our education as children, of our training as adults, must aim toward this absolute question: What are we struggling for, and how can we win against nature without nature being the loser?

It is not a matter of cold reason. It is a passionate involvement in the future of mankind. It is a sensation of horror in the face of the reality which biology is uncovering, an irresistible attraction to what we call ethics—violently, wonderfully, dangerously, courageously in conflict with the laws of nature.

I have heard that in battle men are frequently delivered from anxiety and confusion. That they suddenly see the fatuity of their constant quarrels, their daily worries, their craving for baubles. If man clearly envisions the true, glorious, and terrible struggle in which he is unwittingly engaged, perhaps he will recover some of his lost paradise.